CU00900792

AA

walking in the

West Country

Discover picturesque rural villages, wild moors and exhilarating coastal scenery

First published 2006

Produced by AA Publishing
© Automobile Association Developments Limited 2006

All rights reserved. No part of this publication may be reproduced, stored in a retrieval system, or transmitted in any form or by any means – electronic, photocopying, recording or otherwise – unless the written permission of the publishers has been obtained beforehand.

Published by AA Publishing (a trading name of Automobile Association Developments Limited, whose registered office is Fanum House, Basing View, Basingstoke, Hampshire RG21 4EA; registered number 1878835)

Ordnance Survey® This product includes mapping data licensed from Ordnance Survey® with the permission of the Controller of Her Majesty's Stationery Office.
© Crown copyright 2006. All rights reserved. Licence number 399221

ISBN-10: 0 7495 4848 7
ISBN-13: 978 0 7495 4848 3

A CIP catalogue record for this book is available from the British Library.

The contents of this book are believed correct at the time of printing. Nevertheless, the publishers cannot be held responsible for any errors or omissions or for changes in the details given in this book or for the consequences of any reliance on the information it provides. This does not affect your statutory rights. We have tried to ensure accuracy in this book, but things do change and we would be grateful if readers would advise us of any inaccuracies they may encounter.

We have taken all reasonable steps to ensure that these walks are safe and achievable by walkers with a realistic level of fitness. However, all outdoor activities involve a degree of risk and the publishers accept no responsibility for any injuries caused to readers whilst following these walks. For more advice on walking safely see page 112.

Some of these routes may appear in other AA walks books.

Visit the AA Publishing website at www.theAA.com/bookshop

PREVIOUS PAGE: *Durdle Door in Dorset*
RIGHT: *Dartmoor National Park, Devon*
NEXT PAGE: *Cheesewring, Bodmin Moor, Cornwall*

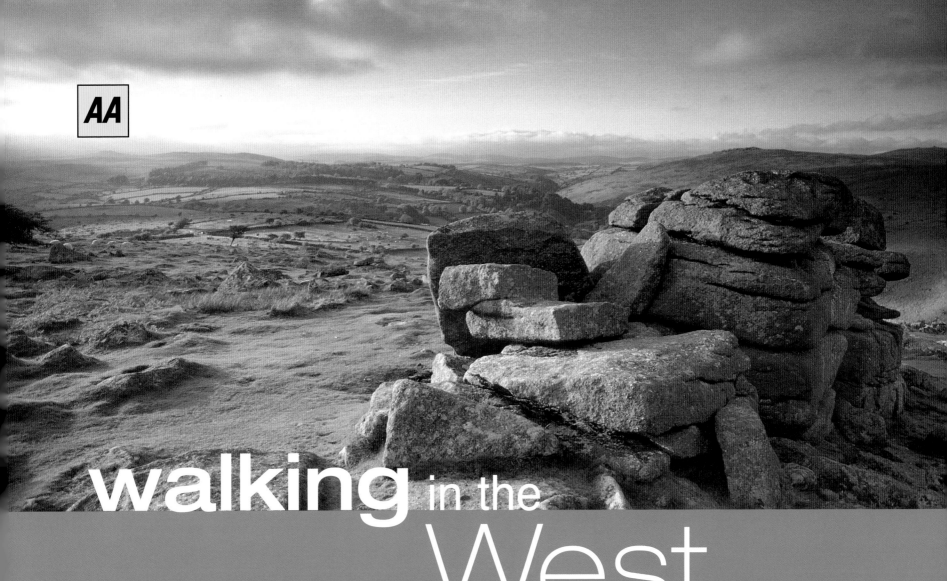

walking in the West Country

Discover picturesque rural villages, wild moors and exhilarating coastal scenery

AA

Contents

This superb selection of walks introduces the themes and characters that define the beautiful landscape of the West Country.

Introducing the West Country

The West Country has two national parks: the wild and extensive blanket bogs of Dartmoor, and the cliffs and rolling heaths of Exmoor. Protected Areas of Outstanding Natural Beauty encompass large stretches of the Cornish coast and Bodmin Moor, and parts of Devon and Dorset, as well as the Quantock Hills in Somerset and the North Wessex Downs in Wiltshire. There are also lengths of Heritage Coast with dramatic landscapes and a rich history. Further inland, the rural landscapes include Dorset, Wiltshire and Somerset.

wonder that anyone scratched a living out of these inhospitable climes. But the ancient fields bear witness to many centuries of occupation, and when the industrial revolution brought new steam engines, the tin mines too were able to eke out an existence here.

The Cornish Coast

Of the southwest, the Cornish coast is probably the best-known section. Crackington Haven draws students from all over the world to study the swirls and folds in its metamorphic rocks. The coastal grasslands of Bude support the richest array of wild flowers in England. Superlatives can be used to describe nearly every step of coastal path, from idyllic rocky inlets, such as those on the Lizard, to the subtropical backwaters of the Helford River and the strategic defence systems that have guarded the Fal and Plymouth Sound for centuries. The coast, from Minehead in Somerset to Studland in Dorset, is circumnavigated by the South West Coast Path, Britain's longest National Trail.

Heady Heights

You'll need a head for heights if you are to make your way comfortably along the clifftops above Hell's Mouth or St Agnes' Point. From St Ives the cliffs face the Atlantic, and as you thread your way along old coastguard paths you will

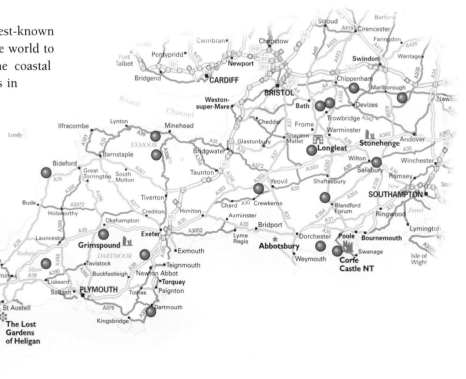

The Devon Coast

Devon's coastal front is split in two. To the south, you'll find you're walking through an intriguing, sometimes even faintly exotic landscape of creeks and charming villages. The ferryfolk will become your friends if you are trying to join up the sections of the coastal path here, and at Burgh Island you'll find they drive the most peculiar craft to get you to this offshore oasis. There are no such problems awaiting you on the north Devon coast. If you negotiate the lanes to Clovelly in high season, you may rue its many charms, but venture from there on foot and you will soon leave the crowds behind. Likewise, persevere to get to Hartland Point, and you'll be rewarded with fine views across to Lundy.

And Into Somerset

Somerset steps into Devon's shoes at Porlock. Here you'll discover wooded coombs linking the uplands with the sea below. Make the most of this, because except East Quantoxhead, it's the final piece of coastal scenery you will encounter in the northern part of the region. Your next brush with saltwater is in the wetlands of the Parrett Estuary, draining the Somerset Levels.

Dorset's Coast

Dorset puts its own spin on the theme of up and down coastal paths. The highest up is on Golden Cap, sitting proudly above 627ft (191m) of fragile sandstone cliff. The rollercoaster effect is perhaps best expressed on the cliffs around Lulworth. The classic circular walk here packs well over 1,000ft (305m) of ascent into just a few miles, as does the walk at Kimmeridge. However, for vistas that include the rock arch of Durdle Door, the Fossil Forest and strata contortions at Lulworth Cove, the effort is surely worthwhile.

And into Wiltshire

Wiltshire is littered with ancient remains, not just burial sites, but the prehistoric equivalent of a municipal boundary, in the Wansdyke, and

using this book

Information Panels

An information panel for each walk shows its relative difficulty, the distance and total amount of ascent (that is how much ascent you will accumulate throughout the walk). An indication of the gradients you will encounter is shown by the rating ▲▲ ▲ (fairly flat ground with no steep slopes) to ▲▲ ▲▲ ▲▲ (undulating terrain with several very steep slopes).

Minimum Time

The minimum time suggested is for approximate guidance only. It assumes reasonably fit walkers and doesn't allow for stops.

Suggested Maps

Each walk has a suggested map. This will usually be a 1:25,000 scale Ordnance Survey Explorer map. Laminated aqua3 versions of these maps are longer lasting and water resistant.

Start Points

The start of each walk is given as a six-figure grid reference, prefixed by two letters indicating which 100km square of the National Grid it refers to. You'll find more information on grid references on most Ordnance Survey maps.

Dogs

We have tried to give dog owners useful advice about how dog friendly each walk is. Please respect other countryside users. Keep your dog under control at all times, especially around livestock, and obey local bylaws and other dog control notices. Remember, it is against the law to let your dog foul in many public areas, especially in villages and towns.

Car Parking

Many of the car parks suggested are public, but occasionally you may find you have to park on the roadside or in a lay-by. Please be considerate when you leave your car, ensuring that access roads or gates are not blocked and that other vehicles can pass safely. Remember that pub car parks are private and should not be used unless you have the owner's permission.

Maps

Each walk is accompanied by a sketch map drawn from the Ordnance Survey map and appended with the author's local observations. The scale of these maps varies from walk to walk. Some routes have a suggested option in the same area, with a brief outline of the possible route. You will need a current Ordnance Survey map to make the most of these suggestions.

the medieval equivalent of factory farming, in the 'pillow mounds' that once formed artificial rabbit warrens. Nothing compares with the ritual landscape of Avebury, where the purpose of the earthworks and alignments of stones remain a mystery.

The county is also richly endowed with manor houses, stately mansions and beautiful gardens. In this collections of walks you can stroll past Bowood House, enjoy the Courts at Holt and walk among one of the finest 18th-century landscaped gardens at Stourhead.

Moorland Wilderness

The remains of settlements on Dartmoor and Exmoor can be traced back over 4,000 years, to the Bronze Age. These lonely moorlands escaped the rigours of agricultural change, and so at The Chains and Grimspound you can glimpse, at least in part, an untouched world. That's not to say recent human impact has not been great on the moors of the southwest. Whether you're tracing the quarry tramways on Bodmin Moor or around the grim prison settlement at Princetown, crossing the great dam at Meldon Reservoir, below Dartmoor's highest peaks, or listening to the eerie rattle of the nightjar in the plantations above Wimbleball Lake, you may reflect on the delicate balance between despoiling and enhancing our environment.

Battle Remains

The region has not been without conflict over the centuries. You'll find civil war stories at Nunney, Badbury, Wardour and Winyard's Gap. At Wells, and many other towns, you can learn of the Bloody Assizes – the cruel retribution meted out by James II's henchman, Judge Jeffries, following the disastrous rising led by the Duke of Monmouth in 1685. The coast is littered with poignant reminders of the Second World War – pill boxes, like those overlooking the entrance to Plymouth Sound, which would have been manned by a pocketful of reservists had an invasion actually happened. The only invasion the southwest has to deal with now is the thousands of tourists who flood in every summer to surf and sunbathe and eat ice cream. These walks will help you venture away into the real southwest of England.

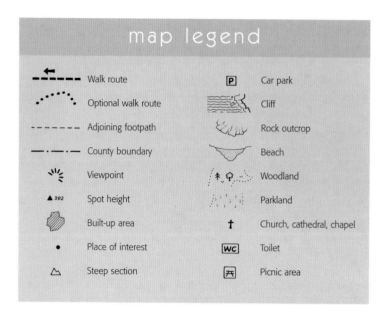

map legend

←-------	Walk route	P	Car park
••••••	Optional walk route		Cliff
- - - - -	Adjoining footpath		Rock outcrop
— · — · —	County boundary		Beach
	Viewpoint		Woodland
▲ 392	Spot height		Parkland
	Built-up area	†	Church, cathedral, chapel
•	Place of interest	WC	Toilet
△	Steep section		Picnic area

ABOVE: *Dunkery Beacon, the highest point on Exmoor, Somerset*
RIGHT: *Charmouth and Lyme Regis from Golden Cap, Dorset*

A walk round Britain's most southerly point, where coastwatchers, lighthouse keepers and lifeboatmen stand guard.

Lifesavers at the Lizard

Lizard Point's far south location can make it a place of sun and warmth, but the sea is still in control here. Offshore, reefs and sandbanks create massive 'overfalls', where, in stormy weather, the sea becomes chaotic and dangerous. On the high ground of Lizard Point stands one of the most strategically important lighthouses in Britain. A coal-fired Lizard Lighthouse was built in 1619, but was short-lived, and it was not until 1752 that a more substantial lighthouse was built. It was first powered by coal and then from 1812 onwards, by oil. Today's light uses electricity and has one of the most powerful beams in Britain.

ABOVE: *The lighthouse at Lizard Point*
RIGHT: *The hazardous manacle rocks, east of Lizard Point*

Lifeboats

The route of the walk first leads to the picturesque Kynance Cove, then winds its way along the coast path to Lizard Head and then to Lizard Point. In Polpeor Cove on the western side of Lizard Point, and seen clearly from the coast path, stands the disued lifeboat house of the old Lizard lifeboat. This was a bold location; the launching slipway faced into the teeth of southerly and westerly gales, and too often it was impossible to launch the lifeboat, though epic missions were carried out over the years. In 1961, the lifeboat house was closed on the opening of a new lifeboat station at the more sheltered Kilcobben Cove, near Landewednack's Church Cove to the east.

The Lizard was also famous for its connections with radio communications, a technology that has played its own crucial part in search and rescue at sea. East of Lizard Lighthouse, the route of the walk leads past the little wooden building of the old Marconi Wireless Station. From here, in 1901, the first wireless transmission was sent by Guglielmo Marconi. The letter 'S' in Morse code was sent from a 164-ft (50-m) aerial, now demolished. It was received faintly – but almost immediately – more than 2,000 miles (3,240km) away at St John's, Newfoundland, where the aerial had been attached to a kite. Within sight of the 'Marconi Bungalow', as the little building is called, is the ugly, white-painted building of the old Lloyds signal station on Bass Point. The original station was established in 1872 to take note of all shipping that passed the Lizard. In front of the Lloyds building is a one-time coastguard lookout that is now manned by members of the National Coastwatch Institution. Just over half a mile (800m) further on is the spectacular location of the Lizard-Cadgwith Lifeboat station, the modern successor to lifeboats that were once stationed at Cadgwith, Church Cove, and Lizard Point. The record of service boards outside say everything about this ultimate expression of the service to mariners by local people over the years.

walk directions

1 Walk past the public toilets at the bottom end of the car park and go along a surfaced lane, signed 'To Caerthillian and Kynance Coves'. In 50yds (46m), bear right at a junction and go along a track, signed 'Public Footpath Kynance Cove'. After a few paces, at a public footpath sign, bear off left behind a chalet and go up some steps, then follow a hedge-top path.

2 Descend steps and go through a grove of privet. Negotiate two more sets of steps then bear slightly right across a field towards the just visible roof of a house. Go over a step stile to reach a surfaced road.

LEFT: *The boat launch in front of rugged cliffs at Lizard Point*

walk information

➤ **DISTANCE**	6½ miles (10.4km)
➤ **MINIMUM TIME**	4hrs
➤ **ASCENT/GRADIENT**	220ft (67m) ▲ ▲ ▲
➤ **LEVEL OF DIFFICULTY**	👥 👥 👥
➤ **PATHS**	Coastal footpaths, inland tracks and lanes. Please take note of path diversion notices at any erosion repair areas, 3 stiles
➤ **LANDSCAPE**	Spectacular sea cliffs backed by open heathland
➤ **SUGGESTED MAP**	OS Explorer 103 The Lizard
➤ **START/FINISH**	Grid reference: SW 703125
➤ **DOG FRIENDLINESS**	Dogs on lead through grazed areas
➤ **PARKING**	Large car park at centre of Lizard village. Donation box. Can be busy in summer
➤ **PUBLIC TOILETS**	By car park at Lizard village
➤ **CONTRIBUTOR**	Des Hannigan

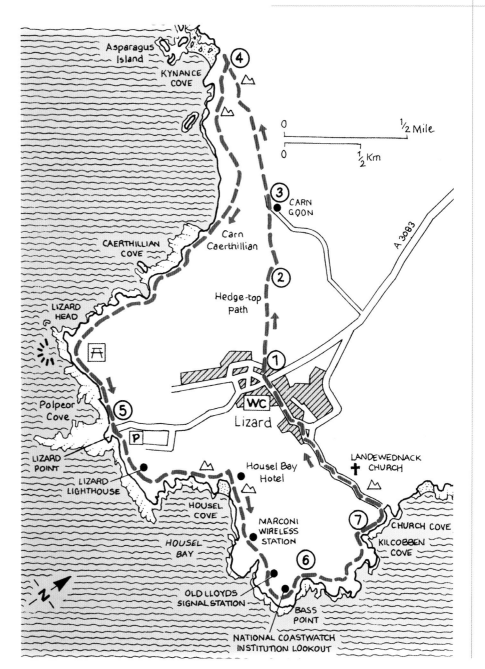

3 Follow the road past the house, called **Carn Goon**. In just a few paces, bear off right to walk along a track. Reach a T-junction with a wide track and cross this to reach the bottom end of the National Trust car park for **Kynance Cove**. Pass in front of a National Trust information kiosk, then turn right and follow a track to Kynance Cove.

4 Walk back up from the cove to where a path goes off right, signed '**Coastal Path To Lizard Point**'. Follow a cobbled and stepped path steeply uphill, then continue along the coast path for about 1¼ miles (2km). Pass above Pentreath Beach and **Caerthillian Cove**. Continue to the rocky **Lizard Head** and then to **Lizard Point**, car park and cafés.

5 Cross the car park and follow the coast path past the lighthouse. Descend steeply into **Housel Cove** and ascend just as steeply, ignoring a link path inland to **Lizard** village. Pass the old Marconi Wireless Station, at Pen Olver, the old Lloyds Signal Station and then the National Coastwatch Institution Lookout at **Bass Point**.

6 Follow a track past houses, then bear off right and follow the narrow coast path past Hot Point and on to the modern lifeboat house at **Kilcobben Cove**.

7 Go down steps on the far side of the lifeboat station and follow the coast path to **Church Cove**. Follow the public lane inland past **Landewednack Church** and continue steadily uphill to a junction with the main road on a bend beside a granite cross and a seat. Go left along **Beacon Terrace** to reach the car park.

RIGHT: *Waves crashing against the rocks at Lizard, Cornwall*

Pheasants and follies – and a different,

quieter way into Clovelly.

Clovelly Without the Crowds

ABOVE: View of Clovelly Harbour
PAGE 18: The cobbled street of
Clovelly, leading down to the sea

Everyone's heard about Clovelly. It's an extraordinary place – almost a folly itself – best seen very early in the morning, or in the evening when most of the visitors have gone home. Clinging precariously to the wooded cliffs on the long, virtually uninhabited stretch of inhospitable coastline between Bideford and Hartland Point, it has a timeless feel if you see it 'out of office hours', or in mid-winter.

Literary Connections

Once famous as the village where donkeys used to carry goods – and people – from the quay up the perilously steep cobbled village street (the bed of an old watercourse), today it is best known as a honeypot for tourists. Most people drive to the village and are drawn into the Visitor Centre car park at the top – but it's much more satisfying, and more fitting to Clovelly's situation, to walk in along the coast path from the National Trust lands at Brownsham to the west. The two 17th-century farmhouses of Lower and Higher Brownsham, now converted into holiday accommodation, lie just inland from one of the most unspoilt sections of the north Devon coastline. Although the walk is rarely out of the trees, you can still hear the pull and drag of the waves on the shingly beach far below.

Literary Connections

Charles Kingsley, social reformer and author of *Westward Ho!* and *The Water Babies*, lived in Clovelly as a child when his father was rector of All Saints Church. Clovelly featured heavily in *Westward Ho!*, published in 1855, and the world suddenly became aware of this remote village's existence. Up till then it had been reliant on herring fishing for its main source of income. Charles Dickens also mentioned Clovelly in *A Message from the Sea* (1860), so extending its new-found popularity.

Clovelly Court dates from around 1740, when the Hamlyns bought the Manor from the Carys, but was remodelled in Gothic style in 1790–5. The gardens are open daily, and there's an honesty box for an admission fee. The much restored 15th-century All Saints Church has a Norman porch, dating from around 1300, and many monuments to the Cary and Hamlyn families. Sir James Hamlyn, who died in 1829, was responsible for the building of the Hobby Drive, which runs for 3 miles (4.8km) along the cliffs east of Clovelly, and from which you get fantastic views of the harbour, 600ft (183m) below.

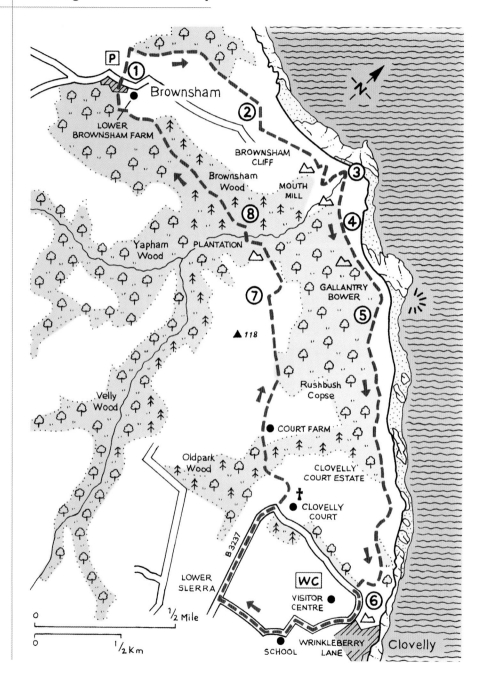

walk directions

1 Leave the car park over a stile opposite the entrance. Walk along the field and through a gate into woods. Follow signs '**Footpath to coast path**' to pass a bench. Go straight on '**Mouth Mill & coast path**'. Cross over a stile and on to meet the coast path.

2 Go right over a stile into the field on **Brownsham Cliff**. There are good views ahead to **Morte Point**. Keep to the left edge, across a stile, down steps and left round the next field. Cross a stile and zig-zag downhill through woodland. When you leave the trees turn left towards the sea at **Mouth Mill**.

3 Follow the coast path across the stream by stepping stones. Clamber up the rocky gully left and turn right onto the gritty track, on a bend. Keep going left, uphill.

walk information

➤ **DISTANCE**	5 miles (8km)
➤ **MINIMUM TIME**	2hrs 15min
➤ **ASCENT/GRADIENT**	410ft (125m) ▲ ▲ ▲
➤ **LEVEL OF DIFFICULTY**	🚶 🚶 🚶
➤ **PATHS**	Grassy coast path, woodland and farm tracks, 4 stiles
➤ **LANDSCAPE**	Farmland, wooded coast path and deep combes
➤ **SUGGESTED MAP**	OS Explorer 126 Clovelly & Hartland
➤ **START/FINISH**	Grid reference: SS 285259
➤ **DOG FRIENDLINESS**	Dogs kept under control at all times
➤ **PARKING**	National Trust car park at Brownsham
➤ **PUBLIC TOILETS**	Clovelly Visitor Centre
➤ **CONTRIBUTOR**	Sue Viccars

4 After 200yds (183m) follow coast path signs left, then immediately right. Go left up wooden steps to follow a narrow, wooded path uphill towards the cliffs below **Gallantry Bower**, with a 400ft (122m) drop into the sea.

5 Follow the signed path through woodland to pass the folly 'the Angel's Wings'. Where a path leads straight on to the church, keep left following signs and via a gate through the edge of **Clovelly Court** estate (right). Pass into laurel woods via a kissing gate. The path winds down and up past a brick-built shelter, then through a kissing gate into a field. Keep to the left; through a gate and oak trees to meet the road at a big gate. Follow coast path signs on to the road that leads to the top of **Clovelly** village below the **Visitor Centre**.

6 Walk up deep, steep, ancient **Wrinkleberry Lane** (right of **Hobby Drive** ahead) to a lane, past the school and on to meet the road. Turn right; where the road bends right go through the gates to **Clovelly Court**. At the T-junction follow bridleway signs left ('**Court Farm & sawmills**') through the farm, through a metal gate (sometimes open) and along the track. Pass through a small wooded section and walk on to the hedge at the end of the field.

7 Turn right, then left though a gate (by a footpath sign). At the bottom of the field go through a gate into a plantation, downhill.

8 Turn left at the forest track, following bridleway signs. Turn right up the long, gradually ascending track to **Lower Brownsham Farm**. Turn left for the car park.

LEFT: Boats in the harbour of Clovelly

A long walk that follows old paths once used when people travelled on foot out of necessity.

Church Paths and Coastguard Ways at St Ives

In the days before better transport, the scenic road from St Ives to St Just, along the north coast of the Land's End Peninsula, was no more than a rough track used for carrying heavier loads by cart and wagon, horse or donkey. Even before this track evolved, people travelled more easily on foot along the coastal belt below the hills, through fields, first carved out by Bronze and Iron Age farmers. Until the early 20th century, the field paths, with their punctuation marks of granite stiles, were used by local people to visit each other, travel to church and to access the market at St Ives.

ABOVE & RIGHT: *View of boats in the bay of St Ives Harbour, Cornwall*

Mosaic

The coastal paths on the outer edge of this wonderful mosaic of ancient fields barely existed in earlier times. They were useful only to individual farms directly inland and were often mere links between paths down to isolated coves. As commerce and foreign wars increased, the coastline of South West England especially, came under much closer scrutiny by the authorities. When 19th-century smuggling was at its height, government 'revenue men' patrolled as best they could the wilder reaches of the coast to foil the 'freetraders'. In later years, the coastguard service also patrolled the coast on foot until there were few sections that were not passable, by footpath at least. Linking these paths to create a continuous route for the leisure walker was the final stage in the evolution of today's coastal footpath.

This walk starts from the maritime heart of St Ives and heads west along the glorious coastline, once watched so assiduously by coastguards and excisemen. This is a very remote and wild part of the West Cornwall coast, a landscape of exquisite colours in spring and summer, and where the steep and vegetated cliffs are not breached until the narrow Treveal Valley breaks through to the sea at River Cove. Here, the route turns inland and plunges instantly into a lush, green countryside that seems, at times, far removed from the sea. Field paths lead unswervingly back towards St Ives, with a sequence of granite stiles reminding you of a very different world when this journey was an everyday event for Cornish folk.

RIGHT: The lovely cobbled streets of St Ives, Cornwall
PAGE 26: Surf school on Porthmeor Beach, St Ives

walk directions

1 Walk along the harbour front towards **Smeaton's Pier**. Just before the pier entrance, turn left up **Sea View Place**. Where the road bends, keep straight on into **Wheal Dream**. Turn right past **St Ives Museum**, then follow a walkway to **Porthgwidden Beach**.

2 Cross the car park above the beach and climb to the **National Coastwatch lookout**. Go down steps, behind the building at the back of the lookout, then follow a footway to **Porthmeor Beach**. Go along the beach up to the car park.

3 Go up steps beside the public toilets, then turn right along a surfaced track past bowling and putting greens. Continue to the rocky headlands of **Carrick Du** and **Clodgy Point**.

4 From the distinctive square-cut rock on **Clodgy Point** walk uphill and through a low wall. Follow the path round to the right and across a boggy area. In about ½ mile (800m), go left at a junction.

5 Reach a T-junction with a track just past a National Trust sign for **Hellesveor Cliff**. Turn right and then follow the coast path. (The short version of this walk goes left and inland from here.)

6 After more than a mile (1.6km), keep right at a junction just past an old mine stack and shed on the left. Continue to **River Cove**. On the other side of the Cove, go left at a junction and head inland through shady woods.

7 At a junction with a track, go left over a cattle grid, then follow signs past **Trevail Mill**. Go through a metal gate and climb steadily.

8 Cross a track and follow the hedged-in path opposite. In about 50yds (46m), go left over a stile by a black and white pole. Follow field edges ahead over intervening stiles.

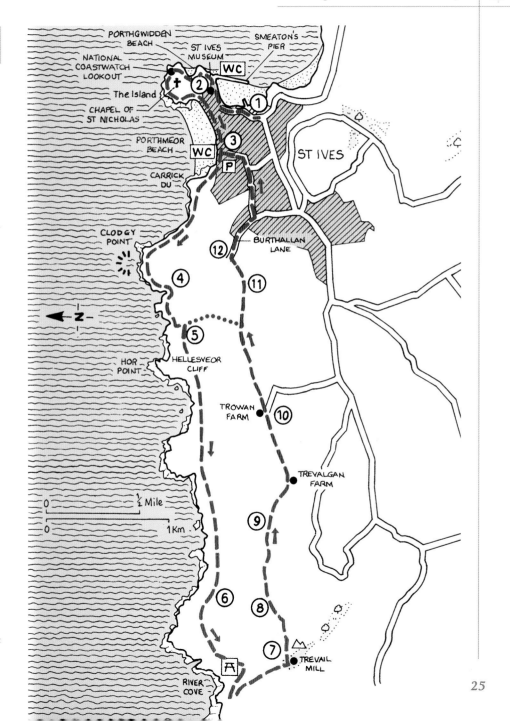

walk information

➤ **DISTANCE**	8 miles (12.9km)
➤ **MINIMUM TIME**	3hrs
➤ **ASCENT/GRADIENT**	394ft (120m) ▲▲▲
➤ **LEVEL OF DIFFICULTY**	🚶🚶 🚶🚶 🚶🚶
➤ **PATHS**	Coastal path, can be quite rocky. Field paths, some stiles
➤ **LANDSCAPE**	Very scenic coast and small inland fields
➤ **SUGGESTED MAP**	OS Explorer 102 Land's End
➤ **START/FINISH**	Grid reference: SW 522408
➤ **DOG FRIENDLINESS**	Dogs on lead through grazed areas
➤ **PARKING**	Upper Trenwith car park in St Ives or at Porthmeor Beach
➤ **PUBLIC TOILETS**	Smeaton's Pier and Porthmeor car park
➤ **CONTRIBUTOR**	Des Hannigan

9 Follow the right-hand edge of the field containing a parish boundary stone. Cross two stiles and at a hedge corner, bear right across the field and continue to **Trevalgan Farm**. Cross behind the farm to a stile, then continue to Trowan Farm.

10 At **Trowan Farm**, go left over a stile in front of a house, then turn right. Go through the farmyard to a lane, then turn left, then right, over a stile. Follow the field paths over several stiles.

11 Go over a stile and through a metal gate, pass a field gap, then go left and down a hedged-in path. Go over a big stile and pass between high hedges to reach a lane.

12 Turn right along the lane (**Burthallan Lane**) to a T-junction with the main road. Turn left and follow the road downhill to **Porthmeor Beach** and the car park. Retrace the outward route to Smeaton Pier.

A superb moorland walk across the exhilarating wilds of Bodmin Moor.

Rocky Bounds of Bodmin

ABOVE: *The Hurlers Stone circles on Bodmin Moor, Cornwall*

Walk across London's Westminster Bridge and you walk across Bodmin Moor. Granite used in the fabric of the bridge comes from the now disused granite quarry of the Cheesewring that dominates the eastern section of the moor near the village of Minions. Bodmin Moor granite was also used in London's Albert Memorial and in countless other structures world-wide, including a lighthouse in Sri Lanka. Nineteenth century stone workers extracted granite, not only from the great raw gash of Cheesewring Quarry, but also from the wildest parts of the moor, such as the lower slopes of Kilmar Tor, on Twelve Men's Moor, where this walk leads.

Cider Press

Cheesewring Quarry is the torn-open heart of Stowe's Hill. It takes its name from a remarkable granite 'tor'; a pile of naturally formed rock that stands on the quarry's lip. The name 'Cheesewring' comes from the tor's fanciful resemblance to a traditional cider press, used to crush apples into a 'cheese'. There are many similar 'cheesewrings' throughout Bodmin Moor, but none so splendid as this one. Such formations were partly formed below ground millions of years ago, and were then exposed when erosion sculpted the landscape. On the way up to the Cheesewring, visit Daniel Gumb's Cave, a reconstructed version of a rock 'house', once occupied by an 18th-century stone worker who was also a self-taught philosopher and mathematician. On the roof you will see a roughly carved theorem, though its authenticity is not proven. Beyond the Cheesewring, the summit of Stowe's Hill is enclosed by an old 'pound'; the defining walls of a possible Bronze Age settlement.

Relics of a much older society than that of the quarry workers' are found at the very start of the walk, where you pass the stone circle called The Hurlers. These are remnants of Bronze Age ceremonial sites, though a later culture created fanciful tales of the pillars, and those of the nearby 'Pipers'. It's said they were men turned to stone for playing the Cornish ball-throwing sport of hurling on a Sunday – to the sound of music. Relish the names, but reflect on the more intriguing Bronze Age realities. Beyond the Cheesewring and The Hurlers, the walk will take you through a compelling landscape, along the granite 'setts', or slabs, of disused quarry tramways, and past lonely tors at the heart of Bodmin Moor.

RIGHT: The Hurlers Stone Circles and the Cheesewring on Bodmin Moor, Cornwall

walk directions

1 Leave the car park by steps at its top end, beside an information board about **The Hurlers stone circles**. Cross the grass to a broad, stony track. Turn right and follow the track, passing The Hurlers circles on the right and the **Pipers stones** further on.

2 At a three-way junction, by a large granite block, take the right-hand track down through a shallow valley bottom, then climb uphill on a green track towards **Cheesewring Quarry**. At a junction with another track, cross over and follow a grassy track uphill towards the quarry. At the first green hillock, go sharp right, then round left to find **Daniel Gumb's Cave**. Return to the path and follow it uphill alongside the fenced-in rim of the quarry to the Cheesewring rock formation.

3 Retrace your steps towards the shallow valley bottom.

4 A short distance from the valley bottom, abreast of some thorn trees on the right and just before a fenced-off mound on the left, turn off right along a path. Keep left of the thorn trees and a big leaning block of granite and soon pick up the faint beginnings of a grassy track. Follow this track, keeping to the right of a solitary thorn tree and some gorse bushes. The track soon becomes much clearer.

5 The track begins to strand. At a leaning rock, split like a whale's mouth, keep right along a path through scrub, with the rocky heights of **Sharp Tor** in line ahead. Keep to the path round the slope, with **Wardbrook Farm** left and **Sharp Tor** ahead. Reach a surfaced road and turn right for a few paces to reach an open gateway.

walk information

➤ **DISTANCE**	3 miles (4.8km)
➤ **MINIMUM TIME**	2hrs 30min
➤ **ASCENT/GRADIENT**	230ft (70m) ▲ ▲ ▲
➤ **LEVEL OF DIFFICULTY**	🚶 🚶 🚶
➤ **PATHS**	Moorland tracks and paths, and disused quarry tramways
➤ **LANDSCAPE**	Open moorland punctuated with rocky tors
➤ **SUGGESTED MAP**	OS Explorer 109 Bodmin Moor
➤ **START/FINISH**	Grid reference: SX 260711
➤ **DOG FRIENDLINESS**	Keep under strict control around livestock
➤ **PARKING**	The Hurlers car park on south west side of Minions village
➤ **PUBLIC TOILETS**	Minions village
➤ **CONTRIBUTOR**	Des Hannigan

6 Go to the right of the fence by the gateway and follow a path alongside the fence, past two slim granite pillars. Join a disused tramway and follow this.

7 Pass some big piles of broken rock and, about 30yds (27m) beyond them, turn sharp right at a wall corner. Follow a green track uphill and alongside a wall. Where the wall ends, keep on uphill to reach a broad track.

8 Turn right along the track if you want to visit Cheesewring Quarry. For the main route, turn left and follow the track to **Minions** village. Pass the **Minions Heritage Centre**, a converted mine engine house. At the main road, turn right through the village to return to the **car park**.

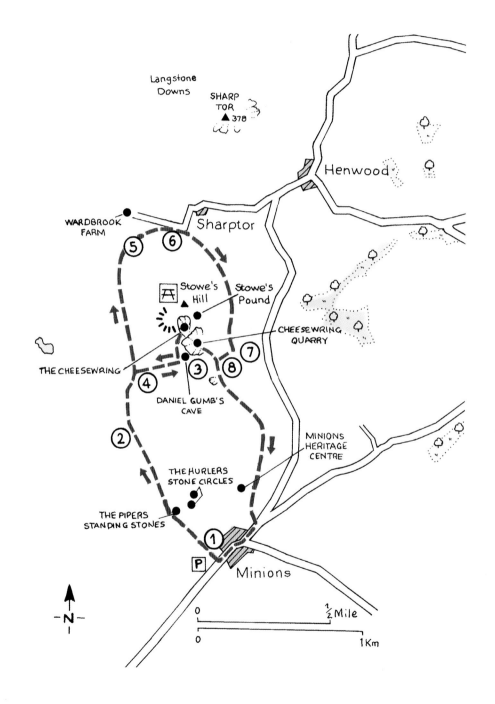

The River Bovey woodlands and the old Newton Abbot-to-Moretonhampstead railway line.

The Dartmoor National Park Authority at Bovey Tracey

ABOVE: *Waterfall at Becky Falls, Dartmoor National Park, Devon*

The signs as you approach Bovey Tracey proudly proclaim the town as being the 'Gateway to the Moor', and although the town is 3 miles (4.8km) from open moor, the landscape changes markedly as you leave the town. To the west the road climbs steadily up towards the Hay Tor, and the northern route travels past Lustleigh through the Wray valley to reach Moretonhampstead and moorland beyond. The town is also home to the headquarters of the Dartmoor National Park Authority, based at Parke, a splendid house set in parkland just to the west of the town. The River Bovey runs through the National Trust's Parke Estate, and provides a range of walks.

Rails to Trails

The 12-mile (19.3km) Newton Abbot-to-Moretonhampstead railway line was opened in 1866, and finally closed for passenger traffic in 1959. A group of enthusiasts tried to keep it open as a preserved steam line, but were unsuccessful. Attempts are being made at the time of writing to open the line as a walking and cycling route. It was closed for goods traffic to Moretonhampstead in 1964, and to Bovey Tracey in 1970. The line is still laid as track as far as Heathfield, 2 miles (3.2km) south of Bovey Tracey, and is opened to the public on special occasions.

Parke Estate

The building housing the National Park's offices at Parke was built around 1826 on the site of a derelict Tudor house, and left to the National Trust by Major Hole in 1974. In 1999, the eleven National Parks of England and Wales celebrated the 50th anniversary of the legislation that established them. The Dartmoor National Park, covering 368 sq miles (953 sq km), was number four (in October 1951), following the Peak District, the Lake District and Snowdonia. Walkers should appreciate the purposes behind the National Parks movement – 'the conservation of the natural beauty, wildlife and cultural heritage of the area, and the promotion of the understanding and enjoyment of its special qualities by the public'. The office at Parke is open for enquiries during normal office hours and is a useful port of call before planning any walks on Dartmoor.

PAGES *32-3: View across undulating Dartmoor National Park*
LEFT: *The rocky River Dart at Dartmeet, Dartmoor National Park*

walk directions

1 Cross the road and turn right, following the signs for **'Town centre shops'**. Just before you come to the the bridge turn left along a concrete walkway into **Mill Marsh Park**, past the children's playground and through the arboretum. This level footpath leads past the sports field to meet the busy A382 at **Hole Bridge** via a kissing gate. Cross over the road carefully.

2 Go through the kissing gate and turn right to enter the **National Trust's Parke Estate** on the trackbed of the, now dismantled, Newton Abbot-to-Moretonhampstead railway line. Follow the path over the **Bovey**.

3 Turn immediately left down wooden steps and over a stile to follow the river (left). Cross a stile at the end of the field and carry on through a wooded strip, down wooden steps and over a footbridge and stile into the next field.

walk information

➤ **DISTANCE**	3 miles (4.8km)
➤ **MINIMUM TIME**	1hr 30min
➤ **ASCENT/GRADIENT**	196ft (60m) ▲ ▲ ▲
➤ **LEVEL OF DIFFICULTY**	🚶 🚶 🚶
➤ **PATHS**	Woodland and field paths, 4 stiles
➤ **LANDSCAPE**	Wooded river valley and parkland
➤ **SUGGESTED MAP**	OS Explorer 110 Torquay & Dawlish
➤ **START/FINISH**	Grid reference: SX 814782
➤ **DOG FRIENDLINESS**	Dogs should be kept under control at all times
➤ **PARKING**	Car park on the B3344 at lower end of Fore Street, Bovey Tracey, with tourist information office
➤ **PUBLIC TOILETS**	At car park
➤ **CONTRIBUTOR**	Sue Viccars

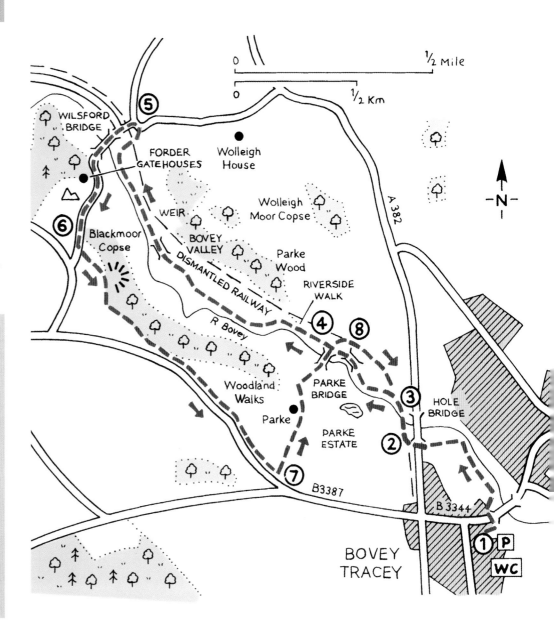

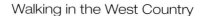

4 Signs here point left for **Parke** and right for '**Railway Walk**' but you should go straight on, following the '**Riverside Walk**' through the field into woodland, then on a raised wooden walkway to the river. The path winds on, then runs along between woods with fields on the right, then over a footbridge to meet the river at a weir. Follow the bank, ignoring a broad track right. Two kissing gates lead out of National Trust land and past a footbridge on the left. A few paces later, the footpath turns right to cross the railway track. Turn left and straight on to a lane via a kissing gate.

5 Turn left (signposted '**Manaton**') and pass between the old railway bridge piers. Walk across **Wilsford Bridge**, ignoring signs to **Lustleigh** on the right. Continue up the lane past **Forder gatehouses**, then steeply uphill until the lane bends sharp right.

6 Turn left over a stile to re-enter the **Parke Estate**. The wooded path is narrow, with views left over the Bovey Valley. Go through a beech wood and kissing gate to enter a large field. Keep to the right edge, dropping gradually downhill, to leave via a kissing gate and down a narrow wooded path parallel to the road.

7 The path ends at a kissing gate; turn sharp left to walk across the parkland and the drive to Parke car park. Walk downhill to cross the lower drive, then left to walk below the house, ending at a five-bar gate. Turn right ('**Riverside Walk**') to cross the river at **Parke Bridge**, then straight on to join the old railway track.

8 Turn right and follow the track until it crosses the **Bovey**, to meet the A382. Cross the road to enter **Mill Marsh Park** and retrace your steps to your car.

RIGHT: *Thatched stone cottages at Buckland in the Moor, Dartmoor National Park*

A view of Yes Tor and High Willhays
— without having to climb them —
and an ancient oak woodland.

Dartmoor's Highest Tors

ABOVE: *Ponies at Hay Tor, Dartmoor*
National Park

If you want to get a 'quick fix' and sample everything that Dartmoor has to offer, but fairly easily and in a relatively short time – then this is the walk for you. Within 10 minutes of the A30 as it races past Okehampton, you can get the lot: a tranquil reservoir, a sparkling river and waterfall tumbling though a beautiful tree-lined valley, wide expanses of open moorland, an area of ancient lichen-encrusted oak woodland and a great view of the highest tors on the moor – and all without expending too much effort. You don't have to tramp for miles over unhospitable moorland or get to grips with a compass to get a real feel of the moor. Although don't attempt this walk in mist.

Black Tor Copse

Owned by the Duchy of Cornwall, this is one of the best areas of ancient high altitude oak woodland in Britain, and was established as a National Nature Reserve in 1996. There is a huge variety of mosses and lichens covering the granite boulders from which the stunted oaks emerge – and the whole place is enchanting. There are two other areas of upland woodland on the moor – at Piles Copse in the Erme Valley and at Wistman's Wood by the side of the West Dart River just north of Two Bridges. In all three places, the oaks have remained ungrazed because the clutter of granite boulders beneath has protected them from the ravages of the local sheep. Black Tor Copse feels little visited and remote – the atmosphere is quite magical.

Dartmoor's Highest Tors

Dartmoor is basically a huge granite intrusion, pushed up through surrounding sedimentary rocks, formed in the same way as Bodmin Moor in Cornwall and the Isles of Scilly. Where it is exposed to the elements, this raised granite plateau has been weathered into giant blocks, creating the tors so characteristic of the area. The highest part of the moor lies in the north east corner, just south of the A30, where it rises to 2,037ft (621m) at High Willhays, seen from this walk. The average height of the moor, however, is around 1,200ft (366m).

Railway Stone

Meldon Quarry is around 200 years old, and was originally mined for a range of minerals. Tin, copper, limestone, roadstone and aplite, arsenic, copper, granite and churt have all come from here. The Black Down copper mine was in operation in the 19th century, as was the Hornfeld Quarry, which produced ballast for the new railways in the area. The quarry today produces ballast, roadstone, concrete aggregates and building stone, and covers 235 acres (95ha).

RIGHT: *Hound Tor, Dartmoor National Park*

1 Walk up the stone steps by the toilets, through the gate and left on a tarmac way towards the dam, signposted 'Bridleway to Moor'. Cross over the dam.

2 Turn right along a stony track. You will soon see a stile (right) leading to a waterside picnic area. Don't go over the stile, but leave the track here to go straight on, following the edge of the reservoir through a little side valley and over a small footbridge. The narrow path undulates to a steepish descent at the end of the reservoir, to meet the broad, marshy valley of the **West Okement River**; the swell of **Corn Ridge** 1,762ft (539m) lies ahead.

3 Cross the small wooden footbridge and take the narrow flinty path along the left edge of the valley, keeping to the bottom of the steep slope on your left. The path broadens uphill and becomes grassy as it rounds **Vellake Corner** above the tumbling river, below right.

4 At the top of the hill, the track levels and **Black Tor Copse** can be glimpsed ahead. Follow the river upstream past a waterfall and weir, right of a granite enclosure, and along the left bank through open moorland to enter **Black Tor Copse** – a wonderful picnic spot.

5 Retrace your steps out of the trees and veer right around the copse edge, uphill, aiming for the left outcrop of **Black Tor** on the ridge above. Pick your way through the bracken to gain the tor; there's no definite path here, but it's straightforward. The right outcrop rises 1,647ft (488m).

6 Return to the flattish grassy area north of the tor. Turn right to continue directly away from the river valley behind, aiming for a fairly obvious track, visible ahead over **Longstone Hill**. To find the track go slightly downhill from the tor to meet a small stream. Turn left, then right towards three granite blocks marking the track.

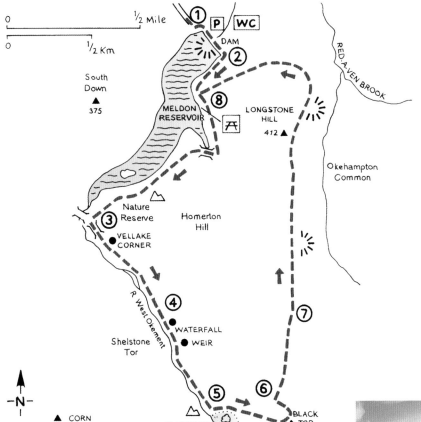

walk information	
➤ **DISTANCE**	4¼ miles (6.8km)
➤ **MINIMUM TIME**	2hrs 45min
➤ **ASCENT/GRADIENT**	722ft (220m) ▲▲▲
➤ **LEVEL OF DIFFICULTY**	🚶🚶🚶
➤ **PATHS**	Grassy tracks and open moorland
➤ **LANDSCAPE**	Reservoir, ancient oak woodland and open moorland
➤ **SUGGESTED MAP**	OS Outdoor Leisure 28 Dartmoor
➤ **START/FINISH**	Grid reference: SX 563917
➤ **DOG FRIENDLINESS**	Dogs can run free at all times, watch for sheep
➤ **PARKING**	Car park at Meldon Reservoir (voluntary contributions)
➤ **PUBLIC TOILETS**	At car park
➤ **CONTRIBUTOR**	Sue Viccars

LEFT: Becky Falls, Dartmoor National Park
BELOW: Yellow and purple wild flowers at Hay Tor

7 The intermittent track runs straight across open moor, with good views of the quarry ahead. Where the **Red-a-Ven Brook Valley** appears below right, enjoy the view of (left to right) **Row Tor**, **West Mill Tor** and **Yes Tor**. **High Willhays**, Dartmoor's highest tor, lies just out of sight to the right. The track veers left around the end of the hill and drops back to the reservoir.

8 Turn right to rejoin the track back over the dam and back to the car park.

An easy round along the cliffs to Blackstone Point and Dartmouth Castle – and a ferry ride to the pub.

Dartmouth's Busy Port and a Spectacular Castle

Dartmouth seems to have everything. The town has a rich and illustrious history and, with its smaller sister Kingswear on the opposite shore, occupies a commanding position on the banks of the Dart. With its sheltered, deep-water harbour, it developed as a thriving port and shipbuilding town from the 12th century. By the 14th century, it enjoyed a flourishing wine trade and benefited from the profits of piracy for generations. Thomas Newcomen, who produced the first industrial steam engine, was born here in 1663.

ABOVE: *Boats in the harbour in Dartmouth, Devon*
RIGHT: *Overlooking Willow Cove along the coast near Dartmouth*

Today pleasure craft and the tourist industry have taken over in a big way – the annual Royal Regatta has been a major event for over 150 years – but Dartmouth has lost none of its charm. One of its attractions is that there are all sorts of ways of getting there: by bus, using the town's park-and-ride scheme, by river, on a steamer from Totnes, by sea, on a coastal trip from Torbay, by steam train, from Paignton or, of course, on foot along the coast path.

Fortified River Mouth

Now cared for by English Heritage, 15th-century Dartmouth Castle enjoys an exceptionally beautiful position at the mouth of the Dart. Replacing the 1388 fortalice of John Hawley, it was one of the most advanced fortresses of the day and, with Kingswear Castle opposite (of which only the tower remains), was built to protect the homes and warehouses of the town's wealthy merchants. A chain was slung across the river mouth between the two fortifications, and guns fired from ports in the castle walls. Visitors can experience a representation of life in the later Victorian gun battery that was established. A record of 1192 infers that there was a monastic foundation on the site, leading to the establishment of St Petrock's Church, rebuilt in Gothic style within the castle precincts in 1641–2.

The cobbled quayside at Bayard's Cove, with its attractive and prosperous 17th- and 18th-century buildings (including the Customs House from 1739), was used during filming of the BBC TV series *The Onedin Line* in the 1970s. The wooded estuary a little upriver was also used for a scene supposedly set in 18th-century China, but filming was unwittingly thwarted by the sound of a steam train chuffing through the trees! The single-storey artillery fort at Bayard's Cove was built before 1534 to protect the harbour. You can still see the gunports at ground level and the remains of a stairway leading to a walled walk above. A plaque commemorates the sailing of the Mayflower and Speedwell from the quay in 1620.

walk directions

1 The car parks at **Little Dartmouth** are signposted off the B3205 (from the A379 Dartmouth-to-Stoke Fleming road). Go through the right-hand car park, following the signs '**Coast Path Dartmouth**'. Continue through a kissing gate, keeping the hedge to your right. Walk through the next field, then through a kissing gate to join the coast path.

2 Turn left; there are lovely views here west to **Start Point** and east towards the **Day Beacon** above **Kingswear**. The coast path runs a little inland from the cliff edge, but you can always go straight ahead to walk above **Warren Point** (a plaque reveals that the Devon Federation of Women's Institutes gave this land to the National Trust in 1970).

3 Continue left to pass above **Western Combe Cove** (with steps down to the sea) and then **Combe Point** (take care – it's a long drop to the sea from here).

4 Rejoin the coast path through an open gateway in a wall and follow it above **Shinglehill Cove**. The path turns inland, passes through a gate, becomes narrow and a little overgrown, and twists along the back of **Willow Cove**. It passes through a wooded section (with a field on the left) and then climbs around the back of **Compass Cove**. Keep going to pass through a gate. Keep left to reach a wooden footpath post, then turn sharp right, down the valley to the cliff edge. Follow the path on, through a gate near **Blackstone Point**.

5 Leave the path right to clamber down onto the rocks here – you get a superb view over the mouth of the estuary. Retrace your steps and continue on the coast path as it turns inland along the side of the estuary and runs through deciduous woodland.

LEFT: *View over Deadmans Cove near Dartmouth*

walk information

➤ **DISTANCE**	3 miles (4.8km)
➤ **MINIMUM TIME**	2hrs
➤ **ASCENT/GRADIENT**	115ft (35m) ▲▲ ▲
➤ **LEVEL OF DIFFICULTY**	🚶 🚶🚶 🚶
➤ **PATHS**	Easy coastal footpath and green lanes
➤ **LANDSCAPE**	Farmland, cliff tops and river estuary
➤ **SUGGESTED MAP**	OS Outdoor Leisure 20 South Devon
➤ **START/FINISH**	Grid reference: SX 874491
➤ **DOG FRIENDLINESS**	Possibility of livestock in some fields
➤ **PARKING**	National Trust car parks at Little Dartmouth
➤ **PUBLIC TOILETS**	Dartmouth Castle
➤ **CONTRIBUTOR**	Sue Viccars

6 The path meets a surfaced lane opposite **Compass Cottage**; go right onto the lane and immediately right again, steeply downhill, keeping the wall to your left. At the turning space, go right down steps to reach the castle and café.

7 Retrace your route up the steps to the tarmac lane at Point ⑥, then left to pass **Compass Cottage**, and straight on up the steep lane (signposted '**Little Dartmouth**') and through a kissing gate onto National Trust land.

8 The path runs along the top of a field and through a five-bar gate onto a green lane. Go through a gate and the farmyard at **Little Dartmouth**, and ahead on a tarmac lane to the car park.

ABOVE: *Dartmouth Harbour*

A long, rewarding walk along the coast path overlooking the island of Lundy.

Around Hartland Point

Although this walk is a little longer – and harder – than all the others in this book, it's a must for anyone who wants to explore all parts of the area properly. The section of countryside to the east of the A39 Bude to Bideford road is often ignored by tourist guides, and little explored – and that's exactly why it is so wonderful.

ABOVE: A lighthouse near Lametry Bay, Lundy Island, Devon

Hartland Point and Lundy Island

Devon's north west tip is characterised by an extraordinary change in the nature of the coast. The cliffs along the coast from Clovelly, to the east, although high, are relatively calm and flat-topped, yet turn the corner at Hartland lighthouse and you enter a different world, where the craggy rocks on the seabed run in jagged parallel lines towards the unforgiving cliffs. You can understand why this area is peppered with shipwrecks. The coast path to the south of the point traverses over what is, in effect, a mass of vertical tiltings and contortions, caused by lateral pressure on the earth's crust around 300 million years ago.

Hartland means 'stag island', although the area is a peninsula, and the feeling of remoteness is made stronger by the fact that on a clear day there are inviting views of Lundy island, rising majestically out of the sea 10 miles (16km) offshore. On stormy days, when the wind is so strong you can barely stand, Lundy mysteriously disappears into a blanket of mist and spray. The island is basically a great lump of flat-topped granite, 52 million years old, 450ft (137m) high, 3 miles (4.8km) long and only ½ mile (800m) wide.

Extraordinary Hartland Quay dates back to 1586, when its building was authorised by Act of Parliament. Cargoes of coal, lime and timber were landed here, and in 1616 lead was brought in for repairs to the roof of St Nectan's Church at Stoke. The quay was active until 1893, and once abandoned was soon destroyed by the ravages of the sea. The buildings, including the stables for the donkeys that carried goods up the cliff in those times, have now been converted into the Hartland Quay Hotel, museum and shop. You still get a terrific sense of how tough life must have been here for the harbour master and his staff.

LEFT: *Rocky cliffs of Lundy Island*

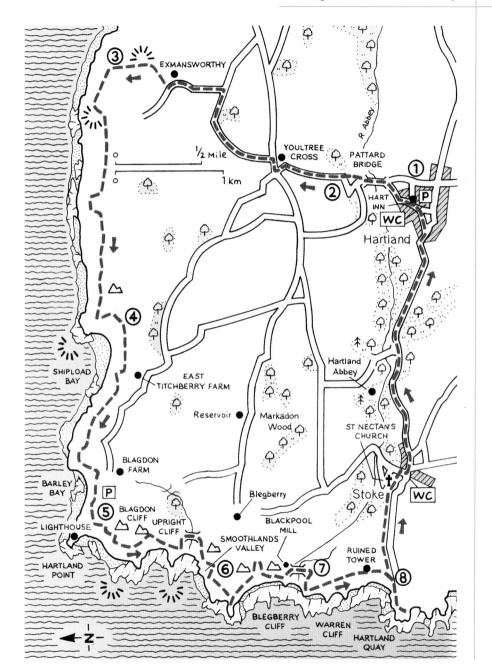

walk directions

1 Leave the car park past the **Hart Inn** (right) and turn right down **North Street**. Turn left down a narrow lane, signposted 'Hartland Point'. Pass **Pattard Bridge** then follow the lane right. Just past a lane to the right, take the footpath sign right up steps and over a stile. Walk up the field and cross over the bank to rejoin the lane.

2 Turn right and right again at **Youltree Cross**. A few steps on turn left at **Moor Cross**, signposted 'Exmansworthy'. The lane veers right; take the next lane left. Pass **Exmansworthy farm**; turn right through the car park onto a grassy path, then cross a stile following signs '**Coast Path**' to join a green lane. This ends at a stile into open fields. Follow the sign left, then go straight ahead to the coast path.

3 Go left over a stile and continue over six stiles, then right downhill. Keep to the field edge to cross another stile. Go steeply downhill, and up over another stile. Cross two more stiles to reach **Shipload Bay**.

4 Follow the coast path through a gate and on past signs left to **Titchberry**. Walk on to cross six more stiles. Turn right towards the sea, pass round a gate then between the fence and cliff, to the right of the radar tower, to **Barley Bay**.

5 Follow coast path signs for **Hartland Quay**. Take the narrow, concrete path leading steeply left, then left again along the field edge (**Blagdon Cliff**) then over a stile. Walk round the next stile and on above **Upright Cliff**. Cross a stile and descend steeply into a combe then round a stile. Cross the stream via a stile/footbridge/stile. Steep steps lead up the other side to another stile. Turn right and follow coast path signs right, over a stile into **Smoothlands** .

6 Climb steeply out of **Smoothlands** onto **Blegberry Cliff**. Walk down steep wooden steps into the next combe and cross the stream via a kissing gate, then up the other side and over a stile. Cross the next stile and descend to the combe at **Blackpool Mill**. Pass the cottage on the right.

7 Turn right to cross the stream on a bridge. Cross a stile and turn right onto **Warren Cliff** through a gate. Pass the ruined tower and at the gate ahead turn right for **Hartland Quay**, if you want a break.

8 Turn left inside the hedge. At the field end, cross a stile and go straight on. Leave the field over a stile and walk past the cottages. Go through a kissing gate and stile, then another, to enter **St Nectan's** churchyard. Leave it via the lychgate and continue to follow the road to **Hartland**.

LEFT: Rocky coastline of Hartland Quay
RIGHT: The Old Light lighthouse stands atop rugged Lundy Island
FAR RIGHT: Steep, vegetation-covered cliffs of Lundy Island

walk information

➤ **DISTANCE**	8¾ miles (14.1km)
➤ **MINIMUM TIME**	5hrs 30min
➤ **ASCENT/GRADIENT**	328ft (100m) ▲ ▲ ▲
➤ **LEVEL OF DIFFICULTY**	👫 👫 👫
➤ **PATHS**	Coast path through fields; country lanes, 35 stiles
➤ **LANDSCAPE**	Rugged coastline, farmland and lovely wooded valleys
➤ **SUGGESTED MAP**	OS Explorer 126 Clovelly & Hartland
➤ **START/FINISH**	Grid reference: SS 259245
➤ **DOG FRIENDLINESS**	Dogs should be kept under control at all times
➤ **PARKING**	Car park in centre of Hartland village
➤ **PUBLIC TOILETS**	Near car park and in Stoke village
➤ **CONTRIBUTOR**	Sue Viccars

*Visit one of the 'oldest' bridges in
the world, set in a quiet valley
clothed in ancient woodland.*

A Round of Applause for
Tarr Steps

This is the longest and best clapper stone bridge in Britain; as such it featured on a postage stamp in 1968. Bronze-Age trackways converge on to this river crossing, suggesting that the bridge itself may be about 4,000 years old. Given that it gets swept away and rebuilt after every major flood, this date for its construction is pure guesswork – or, to use the archaeological term, 'conjectural'. It is still arguably Europe's oldest bridge.

ABOVE & RIGHT: The Tarr Steps spanning the River Barle in Exmoor National Park, Somerset

Cleaca' Bridge

The name 'clapper' probably comes from the Saxon 'cleaca', meaning stepping stones. The first clapper bridges arose as stone slabs laid across the top of existing stepping stones. With a serviceable ford alongside, this one is clearly a luxury rather than a necessity. It's only because the local sedimentary rocks form such suitable slabs that it was built at all. At 59yds (54m), Tarr Steps is by far the longest of the 40 or so clapper bridges left in Britain.

Right of Way

As the bridge is a public highway you could, in theory, be entitled to ride your bicycle across it. (I have seen this done, though not tried it myself.) Quite clearly, the damage you might do to yourself by falling off the bridge could be very serious. That said, the feat is not as hard as it looks – the secret seems to lie in avoiding catching the front wheel in the slots where the bridge top consists of two separate, parallel stones. The ford alongside is popular with horse riders and canoeists, though the Highway Code does not seem to specify who gives way when the one meets the other. It's always very pleasing to see these three non-motorised forms of transport in action together, while motorists are unable to make it down the congested, narrow road.

The Woods

Local legend gives the bridge a devilish origin. Apparently, Satan himself built it for sunbathing on. The shady groves of ancient woodland, that drove him into the middle of the river, form probably the best birdwatching terrain in the country – you need only to sit or stand quietly in the shadow of a tree trunk and wait for the birds to parade before you. It's also good for the birds, offering them safety from hawks and buzzards, plenty of nest sites, insects to eat and open flight paths between the branches.

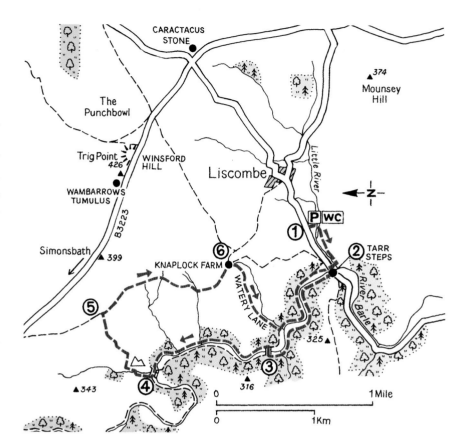

walk information

➤ **DISTANCE**	5¼ miles (8.4km)
➤ **MINIMUM TIME**	2hrs 30min
➤ **ASCENT/GRADIENT**	700ft (210m) ▲▲▲
➤ **LEVEL OF DIFFICULTY**	🚶🚶🚶
➤ **PATHS**	Riverside paths and field tracks, some open moor, no stiles
➤ **LANDSCAPE**	Wooded river valley and pasture slopes above
➤ **SUGGESTED MAP**	OS Outdoor Leisure 9 Exmoor
➤ **START / FINISH**	Grid reference: SS 872323
➤ **DOG FRIENDLINESS**	Dogs can run off-lead along River Barle
➤ **PARKING**	Just over ¼ mile (400m) east of Tarr Steps – can be full in summer. (Parking at Tarr Steps for disabled people only)
➤ **PUBLIC TOILETS**	At car park
➤ **CONTRIBUTOR**	Ronald Turnbull

LEFT: *The rolling hills of Exmoor seen from Withypool*
BELOW: *The River Barle runs through Dulverton in Somerset*

walk directions

1 Leave the bottom of the car park by a footpath on the left-hand side, signposted 'Scenic Path'. This takes you down to the left of the road to the **Little River**, crossing two footbridges on its way to **Tarr Steps**, over the River Barle, ahead.

2 Cross the Steps, turning upstream at the far side (signposted 'Circular Walk'). Follow a wide riverbank path past what looks like an exciting wire footbridge but is, in fact, a device for intercepting floating trees in times of flood. After ¾ mile (1.2km), the path crosses a side-stream on stepping stones, and immediately afterwards reaches a long footbridge over the **River Barle**.

3 Cross, and continue upstream, with the river now on the left. After ¾ mile (1.2km), the path crosses a small wooden footbridge, then divides at a signpost.

4 Turn right, uphill, signed '**Winsford Hill**'. A wide path goes up through the woods with a stream on its right. Where it meets a track turn briefly right to ford the stream, then continue uphill on a narrower signed path. At a low bank with beech trees, turn right to a gate and follow the foot of a field to a tarred lane. Go up this to a cattle grid on to the open moor. Here, bear right on a faint track that heads up between gorse bushes. After 250yds (229m), it reaches a 4-way signpost.

5 Turn right ('Knaplock') and slant down to a hedge corner. Follow this hedge briefly, then take a path that slants gradually up into the moor. After 170yds (155m), a sign points back down towards the moor-foot banking. A beech bank crosses ahead: aim for the lower end of this, where a soft track leads forward, with occasional blue paint-spots. After ¼ mile (400m), the track turns downhill, then back to the left. It becomes firmer and drier as it reaches **Knaplock Farm**.

6 Among the farm buildings turn downhill, signed '**Tarr Steps**', on to a muddy farm track. Where this turns off into a field, continue ahead in a stony track, **Watery Lane**. After its initial descent this becomes a smooth path down to the **River Barle**. Turn left, downstream. When the path rises a little above the river, look out for a fork on the right, signed 'Footpath'. This rejoins the river to pass through an open field that's just right for a more comfortable sunbathe than the busy Tarr Steps downstream. Cross the road and turn left up the scenic path to return to your car.

Combine a visit to one of Wiltshire's grandest houses with a walk across its landscaped parkland and along a disused railway.

Exploring Bowood Park

Like many north Wiltshire towns, Calne rose to fame producing woollen broadcloth and, up until the 18th century, the town had 20 or more mills along the River Marden. When the Industrial Revolution killed its livelihood, Calne turned to bacon-curing and making sausages and pies, although meat processing had been a major employer in the town from the early 19th century, thanks to its location. Calne was a resting place on the main droving route from the West Country to Smithfield Market.

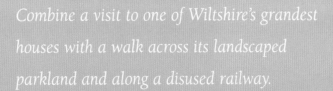

ABOVE: *Fountain in the grounds at Bowood House, Wiltshire*
LEFT: *Orangery at Bowood House*

Bowood House

With little to encourage you to linger, leave the town and the busy A4 and head west to the tranquil parkland that surrounds Bowood House, the true focus of your walk. Scenic footpaths take you through the 1,000 acres (405ha) of beautiful parkland, skirting the lake, pleasure gardens and the handsome Georgian house. Originally built in 1624, the house was unfinished when it was bought by the first Earl of Shelburne in 1764. He employed some of the greatest British architects of the day, notably Robert Adam, to design the Diocletion Wing containing the library, galleries, conservatories, a laboratory and a chapel, while 'Capability' Brown laid out the gardens, which are regarded as his best surviving and most satisfactory creations.

In 1955, the original portion of this once magnificent palace had to be demolished, the Lansdownes sacrificing 200 rooms to create a habitable home and preserve the rest of their inheritance. What is left is still impressive, housing a remarkable collection of family heirlooms and works of art. The chief glory of Bowood, however, lies in its pleasure gardens, carpeted with daffodils, narcissi and bluebells in spring. Lawns roll gently down to a long tranquil lake, and there are cascades, caves and grottoes, while terraces, roses, clipped hedges and sculptures are a perfect complement to the house. If you are walking this way between mid-May and mid-June, make sure you explore the spectacular rhododendron walks, over 2 miles (3.2km) long and not to be missed.

RIGHT: *Waterfall at Bowood House Gardens*

FAR RIGHT: *Deer statues in the gardens of Bowood House*

walk directions

1 Locate the new library on **The Strand** (A4) and walk south along **New Road** to the roundabout. Turn right along **Station Road** and take the metalled footpath left, opposite the fire station. Turn right on reaching **Wenhill Lane** and follow it out of the built-up area.

2 On nearing a cottage, follow the waymarker left and walk along the field edge. Just beyond the cottage, climb the bank and keep left along the field edge to a plank bridge and stile. Keep to the left-hand field edge and soon bear left to a stile. Follow the path right, through rough grass around **Pinhills Farm** to a stile opposite a bungalow and turn left along the drive.

3 At a junction, turn right along a further metalled drive and continue for a mile (1.6km). Near a bridge, take the footpath right, through a kissing gate and walk through parkland beside a pond. Cross a bridge, go through a gate and turn right alongside **Bowood Lake**.

4 Follow the path left to a gate and cross the causeway between lakes to a gate. Keep ahead up the track, following it left, then right to cross the driveway to **Bowood House**.

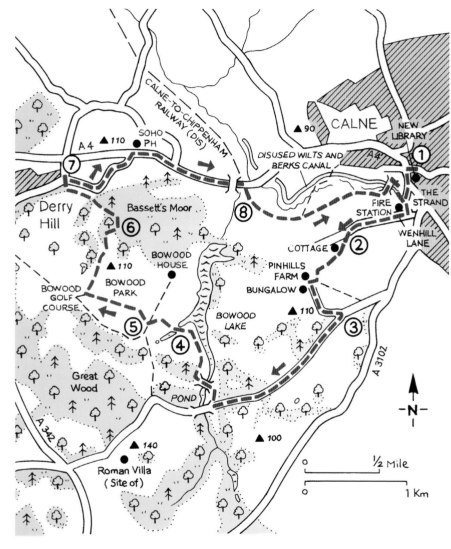

6 Follow the path left, downhill through a clearing (can be boggy) along the line of telegraph poles. Bear right with the path back into the woodland and soon follow it uphill beside the golf course. Turn right through a break in the trees and go through the main gates to Bowood House into **Derry Hill**.

7 Turn immediately right along **Old Lane**. At the **A4**, turn right along the pavement. Shortly, cross to the opposite pavement and continue downhill. Pass beneath a footbridge and take the metalled drive immediately right.

8 Join the former Calne-to-Chippenham railway line at **Black Dog Halt**. Turn left and follow this back towards Calne. Cross the disused **Wilts and Berks Canal** and turn right along the tow path. Where the path forks, keep right to reach **Station Road**. Retrace your steps to the town centre.

walk information

➤ **DISTANCE**	7 miles (11.3km)
➤ **MINIMUM TIME**	3hrs 30min
➤ **ASCENT/GRADIENT**	360ft (110m) ▲ ▲ ▲
➤ **LEVEL OF DIFFICULTY**	👫 👫 👫
➤ **PATHS**	Field, woodland and parkland paths, metalled drives, pavement beside A4, former railway line, 3 stiles
➤ **LANDSCAPE**	Rolling farmland and open parkland
➤ **SUGGESTED MAP**	OS Explorer 156 Chippenham & Bradford-on-Avon
➤ **START/FINISH**	Grid reference: ST 998710
➤ **DOG FRIENDLINESS**	Keep dogs under control; off lead along former railway
➤ **PARKING**	Choice of car parks in Calne
➤ **PUBLIC TOILETS**	Calne
➤ **CONTRIBUTOR**	David Hancock

5 Beyond a gate, keep ahead along the field edge, soon to follow the path left, across **Bowood Park**. Keep left of trees and the field boundary to a gate. Turn right along the metalled drive beside **Bowood Golf Course**. Where the drive turns sharp right to a cottage, keep ahead into woodland.

A gentle urban stroll around the streets
and ancient pathways of one of England's
loveliest Cathedral cities.

Salisbury's Historic Trail

Salisbury, or New Sarum, founded in 1220 following the abandonment of Old Sarum and built at the confluence of four rivers, is one of the most beautiful cathedral cities in Britain. Relatively free from the sprawling suburbs and high-rise development common in most, the surrounding countryside comes in to meet the city streets along the river valleys. Throughout the centre, buildings of all styles blend harmoniously, from the glorious 13th-century Bishop's Palace in The Close, medieval gabled houses, historic inns and market places, to stately Georgian houses.

ABOVE: *Carving detail on Salisbury Cathedral, Wiltshire*

Majestic Cathedral and Close

Salisbury's skyline is dominated by the magnificent spire of the cathedral, which makes a graceful centrepiece to the unified city. An architectural masterpiece, built in just 38 years during the 13th century, the cathedral is unique for its uniformity of style. The tower and spire, with a combined height of 404ft (123m) – the tallest in England – were added in 1334, and the west front of the building is lavishly decorated with row upon row of beautifully carved statues in niches. The rich and spacious interior contains huge, graceful columns of Purbeck stone, which line the high-vaulted nave, and many windows add to the airy, dignified interior. You will find the impressive tombs and effigies in the nave, the fine cloisters and the library, home to a copy of the Magna Carta, of particular interest.

Originally built to house the clerics, the Cathedral Close is the one of the largest and finest in Britain. It is entered by a series of medieval gateways and contains several grand structures in a rich variety of architectural styles, dating from the 13th century to the present day. Four of these fine buildings are open to the public as museums. The highlights are probably Malmesbury House, originally a 13th-century canonry, with its magnificent roccoco plasterwork and an Orangery that once sheltered Charles II, and Mompesson House (owned by the National Trust), an exquisite Queen Anne building with period furnishings, china and paintings.

LEFT AND PAGE 64: Salisbury Cathedral
RIGHT: Stonehenge on Salisbury Plains

walk information

➤ **DISTANCE**	3 miles (4.8km)
➤ **MINIMUM TIME**	2hrs (longer if visiting attractions)
➤ **ASCENT/GRADIENT**	Negligible ▲▲ ▲▲ ▲▲
➤ **LEVEL OF DIFFICULTY**	🚶 🚶🚶 🚶🚶
➤ **PATHS**	Pavements and metalled footpaths
➤ **LANDSCAPE**	City streets and water-meadows
➤ **SUGGESTED MAP**	OS Explorer 130 Salisbury & Stonehenge; AA Salisbury streetplan
➤ **START/FINISH**	Grid reference: SU 141303
➤ **DOG FRIENDLINESS**	Not suitable for dogs
➤ **PARKING**	Central car park (signed off A36 Ring Road)
➤ **PUBLIC TOILETS**	Central car park, Market Place, Queen Elizabeth Gardens
➤ **CONTRIBUTOR**	David Hancock

City Streets

Beyond The Close, Salisbury is a delight to explore on foot. You can wander through a fascinating network of medieval streets and alleys, lined with half-timbered and jettied houses, enjoying names like Fish Row, Silver Street and Ox Row. On this city walk you will see St Thomas' Church (1238), noted for its 15th-century Doom painting, believed to be the largest painting of the Last Judgment in existence, and pass the hexagonally buttressed 15th-century Poultry Cross, the last of four market crosses in the city. Note, too, the timbered medieval houses, John A'Port and William Russel's (Watsons china shop) in Queen Street, and the Joiners' Hall with its superb Jacobean façade in St Ann Street.

Away from the hustle and bustle, your riverside stroll through Queen Elizabeth's Gardens and along the Town Path to Harnham Mill will reveal the famous view across the water-meadows to the cathedral, much admired by many an artist, including Constable.

walk directions

1 Join the **Riverside Walk** and follow the path through the **Maltings Shopping Centre**. Keep beside the Avon tributary stream to reach St Thomas Square, close to Michael Snell Tea Rooms and **St Thomas' Church**. Bear right to the junction of **Bridge Street**, **Silver Street** and the **High Street**.

2 Turn left along **Silver Street** and cross the pedestrian crossing by the Haunch of Venison pub to the **Poultry Cross**. Keep ahead along Butcher Row and Fish Row to pass the **Guildhall** and tourist information centre. Turn right along **Queen Street** and turn right along **New Canal** to view the cinema foyer.

3 Return to the crossroads and continue ahead along **Milford Street** to pass the Red Lion. Turn right along **Brown Street**, then left along **Trinity Street** to pass Trinity Hospital. Pass Love Lane into Barnard Street and follow the road right to reach **St Ann Street**, opposite the **Joiners' Hall**.

4 Walk down St Ann Street and keep ahead on merging with Brown Street to reach the T-junction with **St John Street**. Cross straight over and go through St Ann's Gate into the Cathedral Close. Pass **Malmesbury House** and Bishops Walk, and take the path diagonally left across the green to reach the main entrance to the **cathedral**.

5 Pass the entrance, walk beside the barrier ahead and turn right. Shortly, turn right again along West Walk, passing **Salisbury and South Wiltshire Museum**, Discover Salisbury (in the Medieval Hall), and the **Regimental Museum**. Keep ahead into Chorister Green to pass **Mompesson House**.

6 Bear left through the gates into **High Street** and turn left at the crossroads along **Crane Street**. Cross the River Avon and turn left along the metalled path beside the river through **Queen Elizabeth Gardens**. Keep left by the play area and soon cross the footbridge to follow the **Town Path** across the water-meadows to the **Old Mill** (hotel) in Harnham.

7 Return along Town Path, cross the footbridge and keep ahead to **Crane Bridge Road**. Turn right, recross the Avon and turn immediately left along the riverside path to **Bridge Street**. Cross straight over and follow the path ahead towards **Bishops Mill**. Walk back through the **Maltings Shopping Centre** to the car park.

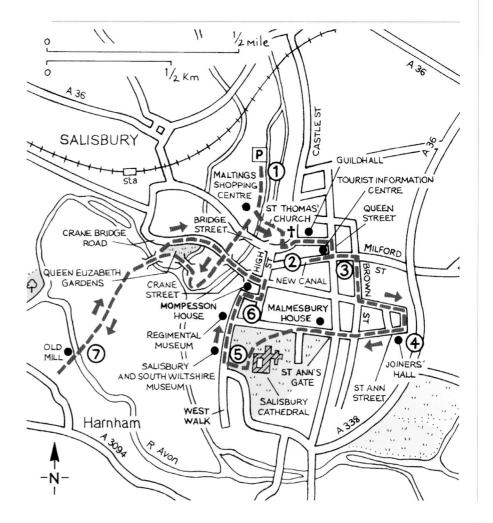

Combine a peaceful walk beside the Kennet and Avon Canal with a visit to Wiltshire's only working windmill and the beam engines at Crofton.

Great Bedwyn and the Kennet and Avon Canal

Situated beside a peaceful stretch of the Kennet and Avon Canal, the large village of Great Bedwyn was formerly a market town. With borough status from the 11th century until the Reform Act of 1832, it even returned two Members of Parliament. It still has the appearance of a small town, with a wide main street, continuous rows of cottages, a few elegant town houses and the flint Church of St Mary the Virgin, one of the largest and finest churches in the area, set in low lying land close to the canal.

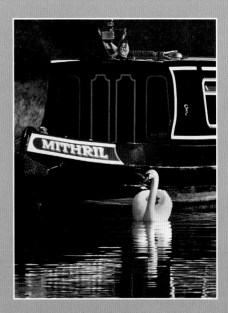

ABOVE & RIGHT: *Boats on the Kennet and Avon Canal at Great Bedwyn*

Kennet and Avon Canal

Undeniably, the main reason most visitors come to Great Bedwyn is to enjoy the sights and sounds of the Kennet and Avon Canal, and the beautiful scenery it meanders through to the south west of the village. It was in 1788 that the idea of linking the River Kennet, which flows into the Thames at Reading, with the River Avon at Bath by means of an artificial waterway was first mooted. The navigation between the rivers had to rise to 450ft (137m) and then descend on the other side and needed 104 locks, two aqueducts and, at the summit, a tunnel over 500yds (457m) long. Construction on the ambitious project, designed by John Rennie (1761–1821), started in 1794 and was completed in 1810. The canal was used to carry vast quantities of coal from the Somerset coalfield, iron, stone and slate, local agricultural products and timber, and to bring luxuries like tobacco and spirits from London to Bath, Bristol and the intervening towns.

Decline and Restoration

Transporting goods along the canal proved successful for 40 years. Then, with the completion of the railways offering faster and more efficient transport, the canal began to fall into decline. Since 1962, the Kennet and Avon Canal Trust and British Waterways have revitalised the navigable waterway by clearing the waters and locks for leisure barges, and making the banks and tow paths accessible to anglers, naturalists and walkers.

Also part of the restoration scheme, and the highlight of your walk along the tow path, are the magnificent beam engines at Crofton Pumping Station. The two beam engines, the 1812 Boulton and Watt and the 1845 Harvey of Hale, operate a huge cast-iron beam and were used to raise water from Wilton Water to the summit level of the canal. Beautifully restored and powered by steam from a hand-

stoked, coal-fired Lancashire boiler, you may be lucky to see them working if you're visiting on a summer weekend.

Wilton Windmill

The county's only complete, surviving and working windmill stands proudly on a chalk hilltop overlooking the canal. Built in 1821, after the construction of the canal had diverted the water previously used to power mills, it is a five-storey brick tower mill and was fully operational until the 1890s. It closed and became derelict in the 1920s. Restored in the 1970s and floodlit at night, you can once again see local corn being ground into flour.

walk directions

1 Walk back to the main road in Great Bedwyn and turn right, then left down **Church Street**. Pass **Lloyd's Stone Museum** and the church, then take the footpath left between the two graveyards. Climb a stile, cross a field to a kissing gate, then carefully cross the railway line to a further kissing gate. Cross the footbridge, then the bridge over the **Kennet and Avon Canal** and descend to reach the tow path.

2 Turn right, pass beneath the bridge and continue along the tow path for 1½ miles (2.4km), passing three locks, to reach **Lock 60**. Cross the canal here, turn left, then follow a wooded path right and pass through the tunnel beneath the railway. Ascend steps to the **Crofton Pumping Station**.

3 Retrace your steps back to the tow path and Lock 60. Take the footpath right, waymarked to Wilton Windmill, and walk beside **Wilton Water** along the edge of fields. Eventually, turn right down a short track to a lane by the village pond in **Wilton**.

walk information

➤ **DISTANCE**	5½ miles (8.8km)
➤ **MINIMUM TIME**	2hrs
➤ **ASCENT/GRADIENT**	147ft (45m) ▲▲▲
➤ **LEVEL OF DIFFICULTY**	👥👥👥
➤ **PATHS**	Field paths, woodland tracks, tow path, roads, 1 stile
➤ **LANDSCAPE**	Farmland, woodland, canal and village scenery
➤ **SUGGESTED MAP**	OS Explorer 157 Marlborough & Savernake Forest
➤ **START/FINISH**	Grid reference: SU 279645
➤ **DOG FRIENDLINESS**	Dogs can be off lead along tow path
➤ **PARKING**	Great Bedwyn Station
➤ **PUBLIC TOILETS**	Crofton Pumping Station, portaloo at Wilton Windmill
➤ **CONTRIBUTOR**	David Hancock

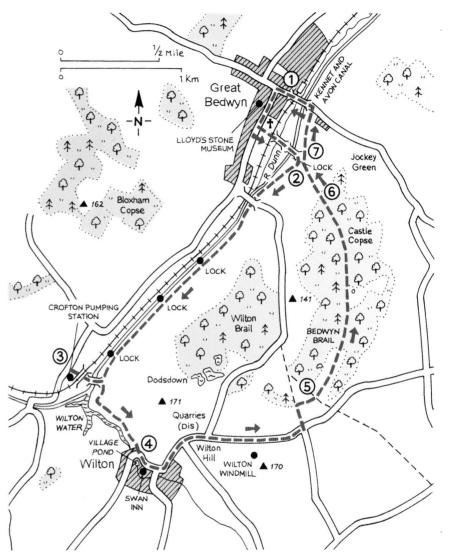

FAR LEFT: *The Kennet and Avon canal at Great Bedwyn, Wiltshire*
LEFT: *Thatched cottages in Great Bedwyn*

4 Turn left, then, just past the **Swan Inn**, follow the lane left, signed 'Great Bedwyn'. Climb out of the village and fork right to pass **Wilton Windmill**. Continue along the lane and turn left on to a track, opposite the lane to Marten. Just before the wooded track snakes downhill, turn right along a bridle path (unsigned) beside woodland.

5 At a staggered crossing of paths, turn right, then in 50yds (46m), turn left, signed 'Great Bedwyn'. Proceed down a well-surfaced track and go through a gate into **Bedwyn Brail**. Continue though the woods, following signs to Great Bedwyn. Go straight across a clearing before forking left to re-enter the woods in the left-hand corner of the clearing.

6 On emerging in a field corner, keep left along the field boundary, go through a gap in the hedge and descend along the left-hand side of the next field, with **Great Bedwyn** visible ahead. Near the bottom of the field, bear half-right, downhill to the canal.

7 Pass through a gate by a bridge and **Lock 64**, and turn right along the tow path. Go through the car park to the road, then turn left over the canal and rail bridges before turning right, back to **Great Bedwyn Station**.

BELOW: *On the Kennet and Avon canal, Great Bedwyn*

*Combine a visit to this
enchanting riverside town
with a canal-side stroll.*

Bradford-on-Avon

*ABOVE: The Bradford-on-Avon Lock
on the Kennet and Avon canal
PAGE 72: Bradford on Avon viewed
across river*

Set in the wooded Avon Valley, Bradford is one of Wiltshire's loveliest towns, combining historical charm, superb architecture and dramatic topography. It is often likened to a miniature Bath, the town sharing the same honey-coloured limestone, elegant terraces and steep winding streets that rise sharply away from the river. Historically, a 'broad ford' across the Avon, the original Iron-Age settlement was expanded by the Romans then Saxons, the latter giving Bradford its greatest treasure, St Laurence's Church. By the 1630s, Bradford had grown into a powerful centre for the cloth and woollen industries.

Wealthy Wool Town

You will find exploring the riverside and the lanes, alleys and flights of steps up the north slope of the town most rewarding. Beautiful terraces are lined with elegant 18th-century merchants' houses with walled gardens, and charming 17th- and 18th-century weavers' cottages, the best examples being located along Newtown, Middle Rank and Tory terraces. The latter is the highest and affords superb views of the town. The wealth needed to make all this building possible came from the manufacture of woollen cloth. In the early 1700s, Daniel Defoe, author of *Robinson Crusoe*, commented 'They told me at Bradford that it was no extra-ordinary thing to have clothiers in that county worth from £10,000 to £40,000 per man'. Bradford's prosperity at the time is reflected in the size of the magnificent 14th-century tithe barn at Barton Farm.

With the development of mechanisation, the wool trade moved from individual houses to large water and steam driven mills alongside the Avon. At the time the Kennet and Avon Canal was built, in 1810, the town supported around 30 mills and some of these buildings survive, in various degrees of restoration or disrepair, today. With the centre of the wool trade shifting to Yorkshire, the industry declined during the 19th century and the last of the mills closed in 1905. The town is now prosperous once again, with tourists and new residents, many of them commuting to Bath, Bristol and even London.

Down by the river, the tiny, bare Saxon Church of St Laurence is the jewel in Bradford's crown and you should not miss it! It was founded by St Aldhelm, the Abbot of Malmesbury, in ad 700 and this building dates from the 10th century. For centuries it was forgotten; the chancel became a house, the nave a school, and the west wall formed part of a factory. The true origins and purpose of the building were rediscovered in 1858 and it remains one of the best preserved Saxon churches in England.

walk directions

1 Walk to the end of the car park, away from the station, and follow the path left, beneath the railway and beside the **River Avon**. Enter **Barton Farm Country Park** and keep to the path across a grassy area to an information board. With the packhorse bridge right, keep ahead to the right of the tithe barn to the **Kennet and Avon Canal**.

2 Turn right along the tow path. Cross the bridge over the canal in ½ mile (800m) and follow the path right, to a footbridge and stile. Proceed along the right-hand field edge to a further stile, then bear diagonally left, uphill, away from the canal to a kissing gate.

3 Follow the path through the edge of woodland. Keep to the path as it bears left, uphill through the trees to reach a metalled lane. Turn right and walk steeply downhill to **Avoncliff** and the canal.

walk information

➤ **DISTANCE**	3½ miles (5.7km)
➤ **MINIMUM TIME**	1hr 45min
➤ **ASCENT/GRADIENT**	164ft (50m) ▲ ▲ ▲
➤ **LEVEL OF DIFFICULTY**	🚶 🚶 🚶
➤ **PATHS**	Tow path, field and woodland paths, metalled lanes
➤ **LANDSCAPE**	Canal, river valley, wooded hillsides, town streets
➤ **SUGGESTED MAPS**	OS Explorers 142 Shepton Mallet; 156 Chippenham & Bradford-on-Avon
➤ **START/FINISH**	Grid reference: ST 824606 (on Explorer 156)
➤ **DOG FRIENDLINESS**	On lead through town
➤ **PARKING**	Bradford-on-Avon Station car park (charge)
➤ **PUBLIC TOILETS**	Station car park
➤ **CONTRIBUTOR**	David Hancock

4 Don't cross the aqueduct. Instead pass the **Mad Hatter Tea Rooms**, descend the steps on your right and pass beneath the canal. Keep right by the **Cross Guns** and join the tow path towards **Bradford-on-Avon**. Continue for ¾ mile (1.2km), to the bridge passed on your outward route.

5 Bear off left, heading downhill along a metalled track, and follow it beside the River Avon back into **Barton Farm Country Park**. Cross the packhorse bridge and the railway to **Barton Orchard**.

6 Follow the alleyway to **Church Street** and continue ahead to pass the **Holy Trinity Church** and the Saxon **Church of St Laurence**. Cross the footbridge and walk through St Margaret's car park to the road. Turn right, then right again back into the station car park.

BELOW: *Town bridge over the River Avon at Bradford-on-Avon*

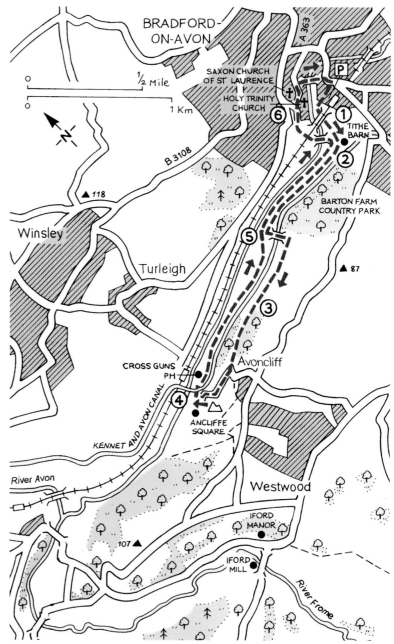

74

A gentle farmland stroll from a rare Wiltshire

industrial village leads you to a beautiful

15th-century moated manor house.

A Walk with Good Manors from Holt

ABOVE: *In the grounds at The
Courts Garden at Holt*

Holt is a rare industrial Wiltshire village with a significant history as a cloth-making and leather-tanning centre. The tannery, founded in the early 18th century, still occupies the main three-storey factory, while bedding manufacture and light engineering now occupy former cloth factories. Holt also enjoyed short-lived fame between 1690 and 1750 as a spa but its popularity declined in face of competition from nearby Bath. The most attractive part of the village is at Ham Green, where elegant 17th- and 18th-century houses stand along three sides of a fine green shaded by horse chestnut trees, and a quiet lane leads to the late Victorian parish church.

The Courts – Wiltshire's Secret Garden

From the green, a walled walk leads to The Courts, a substantial 18th-century house that served, as its name suggests, as the place where the local magistrate sat to adjudicate in the disputes of the cloth weavers from Bradford-on-Avon. Although not open, the house makes an attractive backdrop to 7 acres (2.8ha) of authentic English country garden, owned by the National Trust. Hidden away behind high walls and reached through an avenue of bleached limes, you will find a series of garden 'rooms' that are full of charm and a haven of peace away from the busy village street. Stroll along a network of stone paths through formal gardens featuring yew topiary, lawns with colourful herbaceous borders, a lake and lily pond with aquatic and water-tolerant plants, and explore an area given over to wild flowers among an interesting small arboretum of trees and shrubs.

Great Chalfield Manor

You will glimpse the Tudor chimneys and gabled windows of this enchanting manor house as you stride across peaceful field paths a mile (1.6km) or so north west of Holt. Enhanced by a moat and gatehouse, this exquisite group of buildings will certainly live up to your expectations and really must be visited. Built in 1480, during the Wars of the Roses, by Thomas Tropenell, Great Chalfield is one of the most perfect examples of the late medieval English manor house. Together with its immediately adjacent church, mill, great barn and other Elizabethan farm buildings, it makes a harmonious and memorable visual treat.

Sensitively restored in the early 20th century by Sir Harold Brakspear, after two centuries of neglect and disrepair, the manor house is centred on its traditional great hall, which rises to the rafters and is lit by windows, including two beautiful oriels, positioned high in the walls. Join one of the guided tours and you will be able to see the fine vaulting, the chimney place of the hall, the concealed spy-holes in the gallery, designed to allow people to see what was going on in the great hall, and the amusing ornaments, gargoyles and other fascinating details of this fine building.

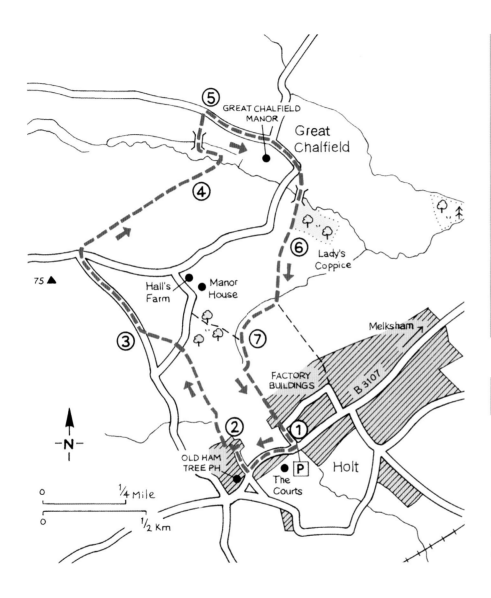

LEFT AND PAGE 78: *Formal gardens in the grounds at The Courts Garden, Holt*

walk information

➤ **DISTANCE**	3 miles (4.8km)
➤ **MINIMUM TIME**	1hr 30min
➤ **ASCENT/GRADIENT**	147ft (45m) ▲ ▲ ▲
➤ **LEVEL OF DIFFICULTY**	🚶 🚶 🚶
➤ **PATHS**	Field paths, metalled track, country lanes, 8 stiles
➤ **LANDSCAPE**	Gently undulating farmland
➤ **SUGGESTED MAP**	OS Explorer 156 Chippenham & Bradford-on-Avon
➤ **START//FINISH**	Grid reference: ST 861619
➤ **DOG FRIENDLINESS**	Keep dogs under control at all times
➤ **PARKING**	Holt Village Hall car park
➤ **PUBLIC TOILETS**	Only if visiting The Courts or Great Chalfield Manor
➤ **CONTRIBUTOR**	David Hancock

walk directions

1 Turn left out of the car park and then right along the **B3107** through the village. Just before reaching the **Old Ham Tree** pub and village green, turn right along **Crown Corner**. At the end of the lane, take the waymarked path left along a drive. Follow the fenced path beside 'Highfields' to a stile.

2 Keep to the right along the edge of the field, then keep ahead in the next field towards the clump of fir trees. Continue following the worn path to the right, into a further field. Keep left along the field edge to a stile in the top corner. Maintain direction to a ladder stile and cross the metalled drive and stile opposite. Bear diagonally left through the field to a hidden stile in the hedge, level with the clump of trees to your right.

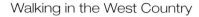
3 Turn right along the lane. At a junction, turn right towards **Great Chalfield** and go through the kissing gate almost immediately on your left. Take the arrowed path right, diagonally across a large field, towards **Great Chalfield Manor**, visible ahead.

4 Cross a stile and bear half-right downhill to a stile. Cross the stream via stepping stones, then a stile and bear diagonally left across the field to a gate. Cross the bridge and keep ahead beside the hedge to a metalled track by a barn.

5 Turn right, then right again when you reach the lane, passing in front of **Great Chalfield Manor**. At the sharp right-hand bend, go through the gate ahead and bear right, then half-left across the field to cross a footbridge over a stream. Continue straight on up the field beside woodland, to a gate in the field corner.

6 Follow the left-hand field edge to a gate, then follow the path straight ahead towards a chimney on the skyline. Go through a gate, bear immediately right to a gate in the hedge and turn right along the path around the field edge.

7 Ignore the stile on your right and continue to the field corner and a raised path beside water. Go through a gate and turn left along the field edge to a further gate on your left. Join the drive past **Garlands Farm** and pass between small factory buildings to the road, turning right, back to the car park.

A gentle walk through the superb

Stourhead Estate.

Stourhead's Paradise

ABOVE: In the grounds at Stourhead Gardens, Wiltshire

Stourton enjoys an idyllic setting on the edge of the Stourhead Estate. Beautifully preserved, consisting of a pleasing group of 18th-century cottages, an inn, St Peter's Church and a medieval cross, its unique atmosphere is attributable to the glorious views across one of Europe's finest landscaped gardens. Wealthy banker Henry Hoare acquired Stourhead in 1717. He pulled down medieval Stourton House, and commissioned Colen Campbell, the foremost architect and designer of the day, to build a Palladian-style house. Extended in the 1780s by Sir Richard Colt Hoare, the house includes a Regency library, Chippendale furniture and many fine paintings.

A Taste of Paradise

Stourhead is more famous for its gardens than the house. They were designed by Henry Hoare II and laid out between 1741 and 1745. Now in the care of the National Trust, they are an outstanding example of the English landscape style. Inspired by the landscapes he had seen in Italy and by the artists Claude Lorraine and Nicholas Poussin, Hoare set out to create a poetic landscape at Stourhead. Having dammed the River Stour and diverted the medieval fish ponds to create a large lake, he began his three-dimensional 'painting', planting beechwoods to clothe the hills and frame new lakes. Classical temples, including the Pantheon and the Temple of Apollo, were skillfully located around the central lake at the end of a series of vistas, which change as you stroll around the estate. You will find the gardens a memorable place to visit at any time, but walk this way in spring for the spectacular display of rhododendrons and azaleas, and in late October for the beautiful autumnal colours.

This walk explores some of the tranquil tracks and paths that criss-cross the surrounding farmland and woodland. Along the way, at Park Hill, you will cross a large bank, formerly the boundary to the original deer park created in 1448 by John Stourton, and pass an Iron-Age hill fort covering 6 acres (2.4ha).

LEFT: *Folly in the grounds of Stourhead Gardens*

RIGHT: *The lake at Stourhead*

walk directions

1 Leave the car park via the exit and turn left down the lane into **Stourton** village passing the Spread Eagle Inn, St Peter's Church and the entrance to **Stourhead Gardens**. (Note: National Trust members or those paying to visit the Gardens and Stourhead House should access the village via the visitor centre.) Continue along the lane, pass beneath the **Rock Arch** and turn immediately right along a track.

2 Pass beside the lake, go across a cattle grid and follow the track to **Beech Cottage**. Keep left along the track, to a stile beside a gate and ignore the Stour Valley Way signposted to the right. At a fork, bear right through the gate, signed 'Alfred's Tower'.

walk information

➤ **DISTANCE**	3 miles (4.8km)
➤ **MINIMUM TIME**	1hr 30min
➤ **ASCENT/GRADIENT**	262ft (80m) ▲▲▲
➤ **LEVEL OF DIFFICULTY**	🚶🚶 🚶
➤ **PATHS**	Parkland and woodland paths and tracks, 2 stiles
➤ **LANDSCAPE**	Woodland and parkland
➤ **SUGGESTED MAP**	OS Explorer 142 Shepton Mallet
➤ **START/FINISH**	Grid reference: ST 779340 (on Explorer 142)
➤ **DOG FRIENDLINESS**	Under control through Stourhead Estate. No dogs in Stourhead Gardens March–October
➤ **PARKING**	Free National Trust car park at Stourton
➤ **PUBLIC TOILETS**	Stourhead Visitor Centre and Spread Eagle courtyard
➤ **CONTRIBUTOR**	David Hancock

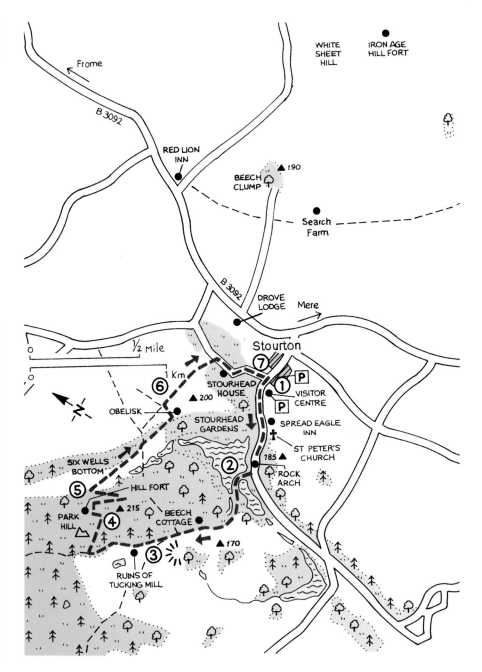

3 Proceed ahead on the grassy track along the top of the field to a further gate and stile, noting the ruins of **Tucking Mill and Cottages** on your left. Walk through the woodland and take the first track right (by a silver National Trust sign) into coniferous woodland. Ascend steeply to reach **Broad Ride**, a wide grassy swathe through the woodland.

4 Turn left to a gate and the Iron-Age hill fort at **Park Hill**. Do not cross the stile, but bear right along the narrow path beside the fence to reach a track. Turn right and shortly turn sharp left downhill through the woodland to a stile and **Six Wells Bottom**.

5 Turn right and bear diagonally left across the valley bottom, keeping left of the lake, heading uphill to a gate on the edge of woodland. Continue up the track to a gate and turn immediately left up the bank to pass the **Obelisk**, with **Stourhead House** clearly visible now to your right.

6 On reaching the track, turn right towards **Stourhead House**. At a junction of tracks, turn right through a gate and pass in front of the house. Walk down the drive, and where it curves right, take the waymarked path left through a gate.

7 To finish this short loop, pass underneath the gate house and turn left up the lane back to the car park. National Trust members and visitors that have paid to enter the Stourhead gardens and house can bear right just before the gatehouse and walk through the walled garden and across a bridge to return to the car park via the **visitor centre**.

RIGHT: The domed Pantheon, built in 1753, sits on the banks of the lake, Stourhead

An exhilarating walk on a spectacular piece of coastline.

Lulworth to Durdle Door

Lulworth Cove is an almost perfectly circular bay in the rolling line of cliffs that form Dorset's southern coast. Its pristine condition and geological importance earned it World Heritage status in 2002. The cove provides a secure anchorage for small fishing boats and pleasure craft, and a sun-trap of safe water for summer bathers.

ABOVE: *Fossil Forest at Lulworth Cove, Dorset*
RIGHT: *Boats in front of the hills at West Lulworth*

Lulworth's Geology

The cliffs around the eastern side of the bay are crumbly soft and brightly coloured in some places, while around the opposite arm, the rock appears to have been folded and shoved aside by an unseen hand. The geology is intriguing and a visit to the Heritage Centre will help you to sort it out.

The oldest layer, easily identified here, is the gleaming white Portland stone. This attractive stone was much employed by Christopher Wren in his rebuilding of London. It is a fine-grained oolite, around 140 million years old. It consists of tightly compressed, fossilised shells – the flat-coiled ones are ammonites. Occasional giant

ammonites, called titanites, may be seen incorporated into house walls across Purbeck. Like the rock of Bat's Head, it may contain speckled bands of flinty chert. Above this is a layer of Purbeck marble, a limestone rich in the fossils of vertebrates. This is where dinosaur, fish and reptile fossils are usually found. The soft layer above this consists of Wealden beds, a belt of colourful clays, silts and sands, that are unstable and prone to landslips when exposed.

Crumbly, white chalk overlays the Wealden beds. The chalk consists of the remains of microscopic sea creatures and shells deposited over a long period of time when a deep sea covered much of Dorset, some 75 million years ago. This is the chalk that underlies Dorset's famous downland and is seen in the exposed soft, eroded cliffs

at Whitenothe. Hard nodules and bands of flint appear in the chalk – it's a purer type of chert – and in its gravel beach form it protects long stretches of this fragile coast.

The laying down of chalk marks the end of the Cretaceous period in geology. After this, the blanket of chalk was uplifted, folded and subjected to erosion by the slow, inexorable movement of tectonic plates. The Dorset coast was exposed to some of its most extreme pressure between 24 and 1½ million years ago, resulting in folding, crumpling and sometimes overturning of strata. You can see this in the vertical strata on rocks around Durdle Door and Stair Hole.

FAR RIGHT & RIGHT: The rocky coastline of Lulworth Cove

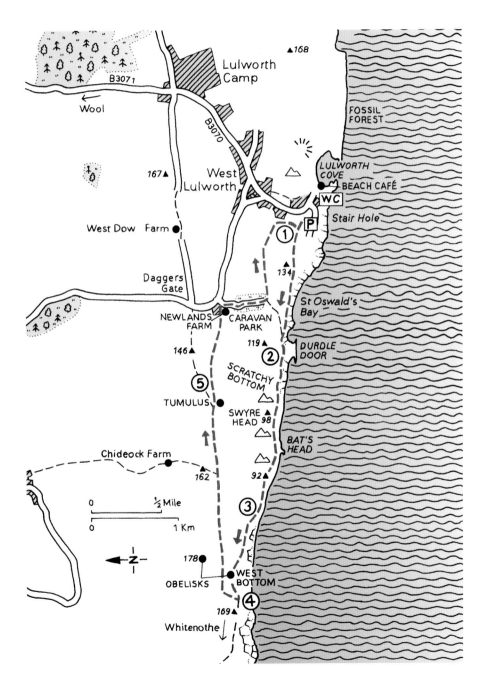

walk directions

1 Find a stile at the back of the car park. Cross this to take the broad, paved footpath that leads up some shallow steps to the top of the first hill. Continue along the brow, and down the other side. Pass below a **caravan park** and cross over a stile.

2 Reach the cove of **Durdle Door**, almost enclosed from the sea by a line of rocks. A flight of steps leads down to the sea here, but carry on walking straight ahead on the coast path and the natural stone arch of the Door itself is revealed in a second cove below you. The mass of Swyre Head looms close and yes, that is the path you're going to take, ascending straight up the side. Walk down to the bottom, then climb back up to **Swyre Head**. The path leads steeply down again on the other side, to a short stretch overlooking **Bat's Head**. Climb the next steep hill. Continue along the path behind the cliffs, where the land tilts away from the sea.

3 The path climbs more gently up the next hill. Pass a **navigation obelisk** on the right, and follow the path as it curves round the contour above **West Bottom**.

4 At a marker stone that indicates Whitenothe ahead, turn right, over a stile, and follow a fence inland. The path curves round so you're walking parallel with the coast on level greensward. Pass three stone embrasures with shell sculptures inside, and a second obelisk. Go through a gate. Now keep straight ahead along the top of the field and across a crossing of paths, signed to Daggers Gate. Go through a gateway and straight on. The path starts to descend gently. In the next field, the path becomes more of a track. Bear right, to pass close by a tumulus and a stile.

LEFT: Looking down on the coastline of Durdle Door, where the weather has carved an arch in the rooks

5 Cross this and walk along the top of the field, above **Scratchy Bottom**. Cross a stile into a green lane leading to **Newlands Farm**. Follow it round to the right, and turn right into the caravan park. Go straight ahead on the road through here. At the far side, cross a stile and turn left, signed to West Lulworth. Stay along the field edge, cross a stile and walk above a farm lane, around the end of the hill. Keep straight on at the fingerpost and reach the stiles above the car park. Turn left and retrace your route to your car.

walk information

➤ **DISTANCE**	6¾ miles (10.9km)
➤ **MINIMUM TIME**	3hrs 30min
➤ **ASCENT/GRADIENT**	1,247ft (380m) ▲ ▲ ▲
➤ **LEVEL OF DIFFICULTY**	👫 👫 👫
➤ **PATHS**	Stone path, grassy tracks, tarmac, muddy field path, 8 stiles
➤ **LANDSCAPE**	Steeply rolling cliffs beside sea, green inland
➤ **SUGGESTED MAP**	OS Explorer OL 15 Purbeck & South Dorset
➤ **START/FINISH**	Grid reference: SY 821800
➤ **DOG FRIENDLINESS**	Excitable dogs need strict control near the steep cliff edge
➤ **PARKING**	Pay-and-display car park (busy), signed at Lulworth Cove
➤ **PUBLIC TOILETS**	Beside Heritage Centre; also just above Lulworth Cove
➤ **CONTRIBUTOR**	Ann F Stonehouse

RIGHT: *View from Durdle Door to Batis Head*

A coastal walk by army

ranges to a not-quite-

deserted village.

Kimmeridge and Ghostly Tyneham

ABOVE: *The ruins of a building at*
Tyneham ghost town

Kimmeridge Bay has an almost romantic bleakness, which the high energy of the surfers and the cheerful picture of families on the beach, eyes down as they potter in the rock pools, can't quite dispel. Giant slabs of black rock shelving out to sea, with crumbling cliffs topped by clumps of wild cabbage, create something of this mood. The slow, steadily nodding donkey-head of the oil well above a little terrace of unmistakably industrial cottages reinforces it.

Kimmeridge Coal and Oil

The story of the bay is intriguing. Iron-Age tribes spotted the potential of the band of bituminous shale that runs through Kimmeridge, polishing it up into blackstone arm rings and ornaments, and later into chair and table legs. People have have been trying to exploit it ever since. The shale, permeated with crude oil, is also known as Kimmeridge coal, but successive attempts to work it on an industrial scale seemed doomed to failure. These included alum extraction (for dyeing) in the 16th century; use of the coal to fuel a glassworks in the 17th century (it was smelly and inefficient); and use for a variety of chemical distillations, including paraffin wax and varnish, in the 19th century. For one brief period, the street lights of Paris were lit by gas extracted from the shale oil. However, none of these projects lasted very long. Since 1959, BP has drilled down 1,716ft (520m) below the sea, and its beam engine sucks out some 80 barrels (2,800 gallons/12,720 litres) of crude oil a day. Transported to the Wytch Farm collection point (near Corfe Castle), the oil is then pumped to Hamble, to be shipped around the world.

In contrast to Kimmeridge, just over the hill lies Tyneham, a cosy farming village clustered around its church in a glorious valley. As you get up close, however, you realise that it's uncannily neat, like a film set from the 1940s – Greer Garson's Mrs Miniver could appear at any moment. There's a spreading oak tree by the church gate; a quaint old phone box; even a village pump. The gravestones all look freshly scrubbed – no lichen here. The farmyard is swept clean and empty. The stone cottages are newly repointed, but roofless. And the church, as you enter on a chill mid-winter day, is warm! Inside is an exhibition to explain all. The villagers

LEFT: Looking towards Kimmeridge from Mupe Bay

were asked to give up their homes in December 1943 for the 'war effort', and Tyneham became absorbed into the vast Lulworth Ranges, as part of the live firing range. It's a touching memorial, though perhaps nothing can make up for the fact that the villagers were never allowed back to their homes. Emerging again, you half expect to see soldiers popping out of the windows, but relax, you can only visit when the ranges are closed.

BELOW: St Marys, the 13th-century Church at Tyneham
RIGHT: Old school classroom at Tyneham ghost town
FAR RIGHT: Overlooking Kimmeridge Bay

walk directions

1 Turn right up the road and soon left over a stile, signposted 'Kimmeridge' – enjoy the sweeping views as you descend. Go through a gate by the **church**, then another at the bottom. Turn right, past some houses, go through a gateway and bear left. Go through a gate below a coppice and soon bear left along the hedge, following it round to a pair of stiles. Bear right across these and follow the path along the hedge towards the sea. Turn left on to the road, go past houses and turn right, across a car park.

2 Bear left to visit the **marine centre** (closed in winter), otherwise turn right on the coastal path to continue. Descend some steps, cross a bridge and bear right, signposted 'Range Walks'. Pass some **cottages**, on the right, and the **oil well**. Go through the gate on to the range walk and continue around the coast on a track between yellow posts, crossing several cattle grids. The cliffs of **Brandy Bay** stagger away to the west.

3 After a mile (1.6km), cross a stile and follow the path as it zig-zags sharply uphill. Continue around the top of **Brandy Bay** on the cliff path. Beside a stile and marker stone, turn

walk information

▶ **DISTANCE**	7½ miles (12.1km)
▶ **MINIMUM TIME**	3hrs 30min
▶ **ASCENT/GRADIENT**	1,165ft (355m) ▲▲ ▲▲ ▲
▶ **LEVEL OF DIFFICULTY**	林林 林林 林
▶ **PATHS**	Grassy tracks and bridlepaths, some road walking, 12 stiles
▶ **LANDSCAPE**	Folded hills and valleys around Kimmeridge Bay
▶ **SUGGESTED MAP**	OS Explorer OL 15 Purbeck & South Dorset
▶ **START/FINISH**	Grid reference: SY 918800
▶ **DOG FRIENDLINESS**	Notices request dogs on leads in some sections; some road walking
▶ **PARKING**	Car park (free) in old quarry north of Kimmeridge village
▶ **PUBLIC TOILETS**	Near Marine Centre at Kimmeridge Bay and Tyneham
▶ **CONTRIBUTOR**	Ann F Stonehouse
▶ **NOTE**	Range walks open most weekends throughout year and during main holiday periods; call 01929 462 721 ext 4819 for further information. Keep strictly to paths, between yellow-marked posts

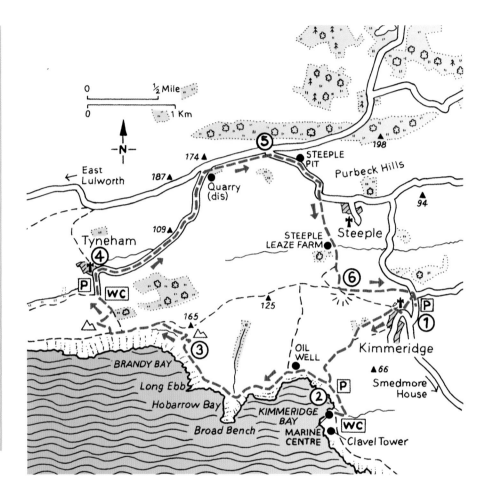

down to the right, signposted 'Tyneham'. Soon, cross a stile to the left and follow the track down into **Tyneham village**.

4 After exploring, take the exit road up the hill. At the top, by a gate, turn right over a stile and go along a path parallel with the road.

5 Emerge at a gate and turn right, down the road, to go past **Steeple Pit**. Where the road turns sharp left, go straight ahead down the gravel drive through **Steeple Leaze Farm** and take the gravel track ahead, leading straight up the hill. Go through a gate and keep left up a muddy path that

winds through gorse and scrub, up the hill. Cross a stile at the top and continue straight ahead, with superb views over Kimmeridge.

6 Turn left across a stile and go straight along the edge of the field, following the ridge of the hill, for ½ mile (800m), with views to **Smedmore House** and **Corfe Castle**. Go through the gate and turn right to return to the car park.

Take the gentle route up a famous sculpted landmark.

Exploring Hambledon Hill

ABOVE: *Hambledon Hill*

The locals would have you believe that you can see America from the top of Hambledon Hill. That's perhaps a little optimistic, but the New World link is not entirely spurious. Lieutenant Colonel (later General) James Wolfe trained his troops here for ten weeks in 1756. Wolfe was already a veteran of the Jacobite Rebellion in Scotland. Tackling the steep hillsides paid dividends, however, when three years later his troops scaled the cliffs of the Heights of Abraham to capture Quebec – and Canada – for the British. (Wolfe himself was killed in the battle.)

An Iron-Age Community

The ditches and ramparts of a fort that dates from the Iron Age encircle the top of Hambledon Hill, giving it a profile that can be recognised from miles around. Today it is acknowledged as a site of international importance for the quality of its rare downland and its extraordinary archaeology. The platforms of 200 huts have been discovered within the ramparts of the fort, offering a glimpse of how our ancestors lived – it is strange to think of this high, peaceful spot occupied by an entire community.

Such a distinctive landmark as Hambledon Hill was a natural choice for a rallying of serious-minded folk in 1645. They were the local branch of the Dorset Clubmen, ordinary people for the most part, who were heartily sick of the Civil War, and particularly of losing out by being caught in the middle of plundering troops from both sides. Their idea was to declare Dorset a neutral zone until the King and Parliament had sorted out their differences – preferably somewhere else. The King, soundly defeated at the Battle of Naseby earlier in the year, was supportive of the movement. However, to Oliver Cromwell and his fellow commander Thomas Fairfax, it represented a dangerous and obstructive nuisance. When the Clubmen, determined not to be overlooked, tried to cut off Fairfax's supplies as he swept through North Dorset, he seized and imprisoned their ringleaders at Shaftesbury.

Home Defeat

On 4 August, some 4,000 angry and ill-armed Clubmen then faced Cromwell and the horsemen of his New Model Army on Hambledon Hill. They suffered a humiliating defeat on their home ground. Around 60 of their number were killed (some accounts say only 12), and around 300 were taken prisoner, including no less than four rectors and their curates. Cromwell locked them up in Shroton church overnight. They were allowed home the next day, after promising not to do it again. After this, the Dorset Clubmen disappeared from history. The Parliamentary army stormed on to take Sherborne Castle a few days later; another decisive step towards their eventual victory.

LEFT: View from Hambledon Hill
RIGHT: The Victorian Church of
St Nicholas, Child Okeford

walk information	
➤ **DISTANCE**	4½ miles (7.2km)
➤ **MINIMUM TIME**	3hrs
➤ **ASCENT/GRADIENT**	541ft (165m) ▲ ▲ ▲
➤ **LEVEL OF DIFFICULTY**	🚶 🚶 🚶
➤ **PATHS**	Village, green and muddy lanes, bridleways, hillside, 6 stiles
➤ **LANDSCAPE**	Pastoral, dominated by Hambledon Hill, outstanding views
➤ **SUGGESTED MAP**	OS Explorer 118 Shaftesbury & Cranborne Chase
➤ **START/FINISH**	Grid reference: ST 860124
➤ **DOG FRIENDLINESS**	Good but some road walking
➤ **PARKING**	Lay-by opposite Church of St Mary's
➤ **PUBLIC TOILETS**	None on route
➤ **CONTRIBUTOR**	Ann F Stonehouse

walk directions

1. With the church on your left, walk up the street. Pass a farmhouse on the corner of **Main Street** and **Frog Lane**. Note behind you the carved stone cross, placed in 2000 on the stump of an old cross. Cross the road into the lane opposite, signed to Courteney Close. Pass a converted chapel, fork left and go through a gate. Keep right along the hedge. Where the gardens end, keep straight ahead through a gate and across a field.

2. Turn right when you reach the fence, cross a stile and turn left. Go through a gate and bear left up a grassy lane between hedges. Pass **Park Farm** and keep straight ahead. At the junction, bear right into **Bessells Lane**.

3. At the end, by **Lynes Cottage**, bear right and immediately left up a muddy bridleway, with a line of trees to your left. At the top, go through a gate and bear left down a narrow lane, part of a defensive ditch at the foot of the hill. At the road, turn left and head into **Child**

Okeford. Just past the post box, turn left and cross a stile. Bear right along the edge of the park, towards the church tower. When you get to the fence, turn left.

4 Cross the drive and keep straight on, with glimpses of the chimneys of the Victorian manor house to the left. At the corner, cross a stile and keep straight ahead down a path. Cross a stone stile by the road and immediately turn left up a lane. This becomes a track, climbing steeply through trees.

5 Pass a millennium **totem pole** and follow the lane right and uphill. Go through a gate and keep straight on up. The path levels out below the earthworks that ring the top of the hill. Go through a gate, emerge from the track and go straight on up the hill, through a gate and across the bridleway.

6 At the trig point turn left to explore the ancient settlement. Return to the trig point, turn left over the top of the hill and go down the slope, following the bridleway.

7 Meet a track by a wall at the bottom. Turn left and go through a gate, with the village ahead. Follow the track down to a cricket pavilion. Go through the gate and turn right, on to the road. Follow this down past a **thatched barn** and turn right to return to your car. Alternatively, turn left at the pavilion, and soon turn right by **Hill View Cottage**, to the **Cricketers pub**.

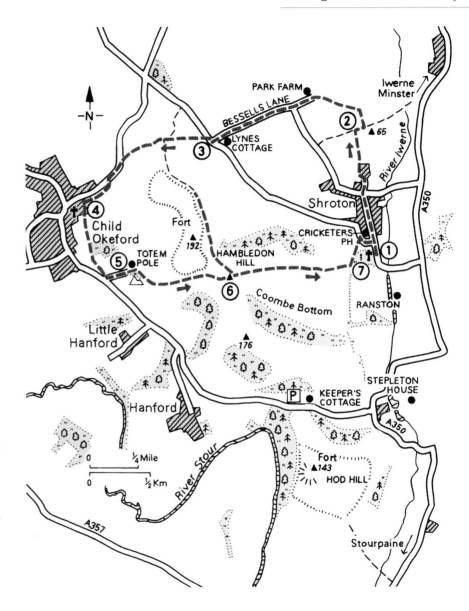

LEFT: Hambledon Hill

Ascending the hill whose
warm-coloured limestone forms the
towns and villages of Somerset.

Golden Stone on the Top of Ham Hill

The yellow limestone, known as Hamstone, found on Ham Hill and nearby Chiseldon, is of a local and special sort. Most limestone is formed of sea shells underwater, but Ham Hill was once a wave-battered, shingly bank. These well-broken shell fragments were cemented together, and stained yellow by a seepage of iron oxide, or common rust.

Consequently, the Ham Hill limestone doesn't have intact fossils. More importantly, it doesn't have the crumbliness of most limestones, or the tendency to split apart into layers. It's what is called 'freestone' – it can be worked smooth and carved in any direction.

RIGHT: *A view across the village of Montacute, and the church of St Catherine*

Romans in the Stone

Traces of early quarrying get dug up and carried away by later quarrying. However, we do know that the Romans quarried here: a Roman coffin made of Ham Hill stone is in the museum at Dorchester. However, it was much later, in the Middle Ages, that the quarries became the making of Somerset – literally. The more important buildings – Montacute House, Sherborne Abbey, Wells Cathedral and many manor houses – were built of Hamstone.

Because of the cost of hauling the stones, in the days before real roads, buildings such as parish churches used the local stone for masonry, but Hamstone for the corners and the tricky bits round the windows. The Yeo and the Parrett provided river transport, and Hamstone could be floated up the Tone to Taunton and Wellington. All over Somerset, it's a golden thread running through the richly varied building fabric. Another quality of Hamstone is apparent at Bath, where they had their own sort of freestone and didn't need to use it. The Bathstone, an oolitic limestone, is crumbling in today's polluted atmosphere. The Hamstone, a sort of natural concrete, is more robust. The quarries were worked by hand, using wedges and a type of pick called a 'jadd'. The tremendous labour of lifting the rough-shaped blocks out of the quarries was a spur to ingenuity and mechanical contrivance. Steam-powered cranes came to Ham Hill in the 18th century but, even so, the work was dangerous, with quarrymen injured or crushed to death every year.

Two of the quarries have re-opened. They are being worked in the traditional way, but the fork-lift truck provides a safer alternative to the block-and-tackle or steam crane. The stone goes for restoration work and also for new building. Cheap transport in the 20th century meant stone for a fancy façade could come from Spain or even China, but today planners are realising that the local stone is an important aspect of Somerset's character and charm.

walk directions

1 Turn right out of the car park (so that the big, westward view is on the right) and follow the road to a junction. Bear left for 35yds (32m), then take a path on the right, signed 'Norton Sub Hamdon'. This leads through woods around the side of **Ham Hill**, keeping at the same level, just below the rim, all the way round. When open field appears ahead, turn right, downhill. Ignore a first gate on the left and continue to a second gate.

2 Descend grassland into a small valley with the hummocks of the medieval village of **Witcombe**. Head up the valley floor, passing to the left of a willow clump. A grassy path climbs the right-hand side of the valley to a field corner. Here, turn left on a track that leads to a lane near **Batemoor Barn**.

3 **Hollow Lane** descends directly opposite. A stile just to its right lets you pass along the field edges, then into a wood. Just twenty paces on, turn right to a stile. A clear path runs just below the top of the wood, then down to the edge of **Montacute** village. Turn left near the entrance to **Montacute House**, to reach the **King's Arms** inn.

4 Turn left, past the church, and after a duck pond, turn right on a permissive path. A kissing gate leads to the base of **St Michael's Hill**. Turn left for 150yds (139m), to a stile into the woods.

5 The path ahead is arduous. For a gentler way up the hill, turn left around its base to meet the descending track. Otherwise, head slightly left up a very steep path, to join the same track just below the summit **tower**. The tower is open and its spiral staircase is well worth the climb. Descend the spiralling track to the gate at the hill's foot.

BELOW: Montacute House built in the 16th-century of golden Ham stone

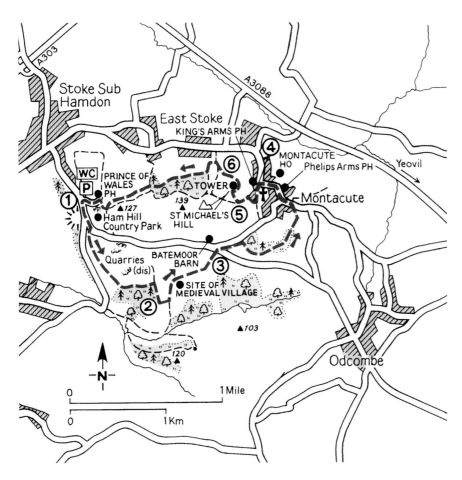

	walk information
➤ **DISTANCE**	4 miles (6.4km)
➤ **MINIMUM TIME**	2hrs
➤ **ASCENT/GRADIENT**	700ft (210m) ▲▲ ▲ ▲
➤ **LEVEL OF DIFFICULTY**	🚶🚶 🚶 🚶
➤ **PATHS**	Well-trodden and sometimes muddy, 5 stiles
➤ **LANDSCAPE**	Steep-sided, wooded hill
➤ **SUGGESTED MAP**	OS Explorer 129 Yeovil & Sherborne
➤ **START/FINISH**	Grid reference: ST 478167
➤ **DOG FRIENDLINESS**	Dogs under control welcome on Ham Hill itself, may need leads elsewhere
➤ **PARKING**	Main car park on western escarpment of Ham Hill
➤ **PUBLIC TOILETS**	At Ranger Hut near start, and at Stoke Sub Hamden
➤ **CONTRIBUTOR**	Ronald Turnbull

BELOW: *Tall war memorial on Ham Hill*

6 Turn half-right and go straight down the field to a gate that leads on to a track corner. Turn left and follow the track round the field corner. After 90yds (82m), take a right fork. The earth track runs close to the foot of the woods, passing the ruins of a pump house, and diminishing to a path; it then climbs steps to join a higher one. Turn right to continue close to the foot of the woods until the path emerges at a gate after 500yds (457m). Steps lead up to the **Prince of Wales** pub. Turn left along its lane, passing through the hummocks of former quarries, to the car park.

105

*On the trail of Exmoor's red deer, in the
woodlands under Dunkery Beacon.*

Horner's Corners

Horner takes its name from the Saxon 'hwrnwr', a wonderfully expressive word meaning snorer, that here describes the rumble of the stream in its enclosed valley. Above the treetops, Webber's Post is a splendid viewpoint out across the Bristol Channel. What Mr Webber stood there to view, though, was the hunting of red deer.

*ABOVE: Walkers amongst the
heather on Exmoor*
*LEFT: A view of Exmoor National
Park from Dunkery Beacon*

The Exmoor Stag

The herd on Exmoor numbers several thousand. Although this is small compared to those in the Scottish Highlands, the Exmoor stag is the UK's biggest wild deer. On Exmoor, as in the rest of Northern Europe outside Scotland, the deer remains a forest animal. Exmoor's mix of impenetrable woodland with areas of open grazing, even with all its houses, farms and fields, remains good deer country.

The calf is born dappled, for camouflage under the trees, and lies in shelter during the day while the hind feeds. If you do come across a deer calf, leave it alone – it hasn't been abandoned. During the summer, the stags and hinds run in separate herds. In the Scottish Highlands deer graze on high ground during the day to escape from midges, and descend to the forest at night; on Exmoor, the main annoying pest is the human, so the deer graze the moor at dawn and dusk, and spend the day in the trees.

BELOW: Valley of the Rocks, Lynton, Exmoor
RIGHT: A thatcher thatching in Porlock Wier, Exmoor

Stag Nights

In September and October comes the spectacular rut, when stags roar defiance at each other, and, if that fails, do battle with antlers for mating privileges. During this time they eat only occasionally, fight a lot and mate as often as possible. The stag with a mighty roar and a hard head can gather a harem of a dozen hinds. Your best chance of seeing one is very early or very late in the day – or else in the forest. I have had a bramble patch beside my path suddenly start bouncing around like an angry saucepan of milk, until, after ten seconds, a half-grown calf burst out of the middle of it and ran away. You may well smell the deer, even though it probably smelled you first and has already gone quietly away. Look closely, too, at the small brown cows two fields away – they may well be deer. I've seen grazing deer from a train window just five minutes out of Taunton Station, though they were the smaller roe.

walk directions

1 Leave the National Trust car park in Horner village past the toilets and turn right, to the track leading into **Horner Wood**. This crosses a bridge and passes a field before rejoining **Horner Water**. You can take a footpath alongside the stream instead of the track; they lead to the same place. Ignore the first footbridge, and continue along the obvious track to where a sign, '**Dunkery Beacon**', points off to the left towards a second footbridge.

2 Ignore this footbridge as well. Keep on the track for another 100yds (91m), then fork left on a path alongside **West Water**. This rejoins the track and, after another ½ mile (800m) a bridleway sign points back to the right. Here, look down to the left for a footbridge. For me this was a thrilling balancing act on two girders – but the rebuilding of the bridge (swept away in floods in 2001) has now been completed.

3 Cross, on to a path that slants up to the right. After 200yds (183m), turn left into a smaller path that turns uphill alongside **Prickslade Combe**. The path reaches the combe's little stream at a cross-path, with the wood top visible above. Here, turn left, across the stream, on a path contouring through the top of the wood. It emerges into the open and arrives at a tree with a bench and a fine view over the top of the woodlands to **Porlock Bay**.

4 Continue ahead on a grassy track, with the car park of **Webber's Post** clearly visible ahead. Alas, the deep valley of the **East Water** lies between you and your destination. So, turn down left on a clear path back into birchwoods. This zig-zags down to meet a larger track in the valley bottom.

LEFT: Descending a rock face at Valley of Rocks, Exmoor

5 Turn downstream, crossing a footbridge over the **East Water**, beside a ford. After about 60yds (55m), bear right on to an ascending path. At the top of the steep section, turn right on a small, sunken path that climbs gently to **Webber's Post** car park.

6 Walk to the left, round the car park, to a path marked 'Permitted Bridleway' to **Horner**. (Do not take the pink-surfaced, easy-access path immediately to the right.) After 80yds (73m), bear left on to a wider footpath. Keep ahead down a wide, gentle spur, with the deep valley of the **Horner Water** on your left. As the spur steepens, the footpath meets a crossing track, signposted '**Windsor Path**'.

7 Turn right for perhaps 30 paces, then take a descending path, signposted '**Horner**'. Narrow at first, this widens and finally meets a wide, horse-mangled track with wooden steps; turn left down this into **Horner**.

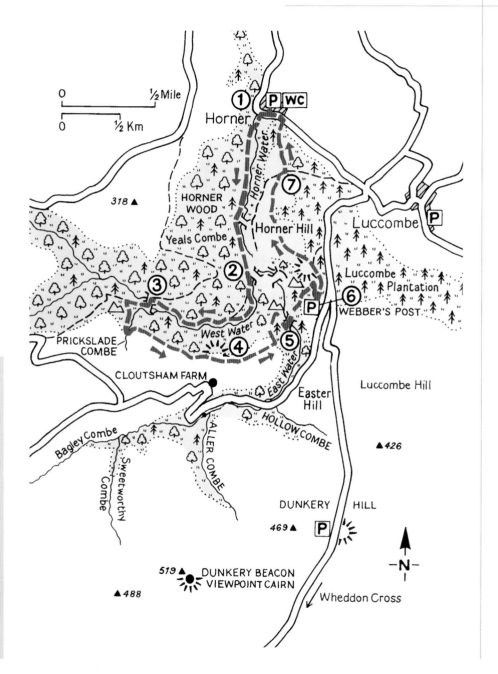

walk information

➤ **DISTANCE**	4½ miles (7.2km)
➤ **MINIMUM TIME**	2hrs 30min
➤ **ASCENT/GRADIENT**	1,000ft (300m) ▲ ▲ ▲
➤ **LEVEL OF DIFFICULTY**	🚶🚶🚶
➤ **PATHS**	Broad paths, with some stonier ones, steep in places, no stiles
➤ **LANDSCAPE**	Dense woodland in steep-sided stream valleys
➤ **SUGGESTED MAP**	OS Outdoor Leisure 9 Exmoor
➤ **START/FINISH**	Grid reference: SS 898455
➤ **DOG FRIENDLINESS**	Off lead, but be aware of deer and horse-riders
➤ **PARKING**	National Trust car park (free) at Horner
➤ **PUBLIC TOILETS**	At car park
➤ **CONTRIBUTOR**	Ronald Turnbull

Walking in Safety

All these walks are suitable for any reasonably fit person, but less experienced walkers should try the easier walks first. Route finding is usually straightforward, but you will find that an Ordnance Survey map is a useful addition to the route maps and descriptions.

Risks

Although each walk here has been researched with a view to minimising the risks to the walkers who follow its route, no walk in the countryside can be considered to be completely free from risk. Walking in the outdoors will always require a degree of common sense and judgement to ensure that it is as safe as possible.

- Be particularly careful on cliff paths and in upland terrain, where the consequences of a slip can be very serious.
- Remember to always check tidal conditions before setting off for a walk along the seashore.
- Some sections of route are by, or cross, busy roads. Take care and remember traffic is a danger, even on minor country lanes.
- Be careful around farmyard machinery and livestock, especially if you have children with you.
- Be aware of the consequences of changes in the weather and check the forecast before you set out. Carry spare clothing and a torch if you are walking in the winter months. Remember, the weather can change very quickly at any time of the year, and in moorland and heathland areas, mist and fog can make route finding much harder. Don't set out in these conditions unless you are confident of your navigation skills in poor visibility. In summer, remember to take account of the heat and sun; wear a hat and sunscreen, and carry spare water.
- On walks away from centres of population, you should carry a whistle and survival bag. If you do have an accident requiring the emergency services, make a note of your position as accurately as possible and dial 999.

Acknowledgements

All photographs are held in the Association's own picture library (AA World Photo Library) and were taken by the following photographers:

2/3 Rick Czaja; 5 Andrew Lawson; 6 Roger Moss; 7bl Caroline Jones; 7bc Caroline Jones; 7bc Caroline Jones; 7br Caroline Jones; 10 Peter Baker; 11 Rick Czaja; 12 R Tennison; 13 R Tennison; 14 Caroline Jones; 16 Richard Ireland; 17 Caroline Jones; 18/19 Peter Baker; 21 Tom Teegan; 22 Caroline Jones; 23 Richard Ireland; 24 Caroline Jones; 26 Caroline Jones; 27 Caroline Jones; 28/29 R. Tenison; 31 Caroline Jones; 32/33 Andrew Lawson; 34 Peter Baker; 36 AA; 37 Caroline Jones; 38/39 Peter Baker; 40 Caroline Jones; 41 Caroline Jones; 42 John O'Carroll; 43 Wyn Voysey; 44 Wyn Voysey; 46 Caroline Jones; 47 Roger Moss; 48 Roger Moss; 49 Roger Moss; 50 Caroline Jones; 51l Roger Moss; 51r Rob Moore; 52 Roger Moss; 53 Wyn Voysey; 54 Roger Moss; 55 Wyn Voysey; 56 Caroline Jones; 57 Caroline Jones; 58 Caroline Jones; 59 Caroline Jones; 61 Caroline Jones; 62 Caroline Jones; 63 Eric Meacher; 64 S & O Mathews; 66 Steve Day; 67 Steve Day; 68 Derek Forss; 69 Derek Forss; 70 Steve Day; 71 Caroline Jones; 72-73 Caroline Jones; 74 Caroline Jones; 75 Richard Ireland; 76 Richard Ireland; 78 Richard Ireland; 79 Wyn Voysey; 80l Wyn Voysey; 81 Wyn Voysey; 83 Rich Newton; 84 Richard Ireland; 85 Peter Baker; 86l Richard Ireland; 86/87 Richard Ireland; 88 Max Jourdan; 90 Max Jourdan; 91 Max Jourdan; 92/93 Richard Ireland; 94 Max Jourdan; 95l Max Jourdan; 95r S & O Mathews; 97 Roy Rainford; 98 Roy Rainford; 99 Roy Rainford; 100 Roy Rainford; 102 Wyn Voysey; 103 Steve Day; 104 Peter Baker; 105 Neil Ray; 106 Andrew Lawson; 107 Roger Moss; 108 Caroline Jones; 109 Andrew Lawson; 110 Caroline Jones